Series / Number 07-016

P9-DXM-785

EXPLORATORY DATA ANALYSIS

FREDERICK HARTWIG
Union College

with **BRIAN E. DEARING**
General Electric Company

SAGE PUBLICATIONS
The International Professional Publishers
Newbury Park   London   New Delhi

Copyright © 1979 by Sage Publications, Inc.

Printed in the United States of America

All rights reserved. No part of this book may be reproduced
or utilized in any form or by any means, electronic or mechanical,
including photocopying, recording, or by any
information storage and retrieval system, without permission in writing
from the publisher.

For information address:

SAGE Publications, Inc.
2455 Teller Road
Newbury Park, California 91320

SAGE Publications Ltd.
6 Bonhill Street
London EC2A 4PU
United Kingdom

SAGE Publications India Pvt. Ltd.
M-32 Market
Greater Kailash I
New Delhi 110 048 India

International Standard Book Number 0-8039-1370-2

Library of Congress Catalog Card No. L.C. 79-67621

93 94 95 25 24 23 22 21 20 19 18 17 16

When citing a professional paper, please use the proper form. Remember to cite the correct
Sage University Paper series title and include the paper number. One of the two following
formats can be adapted (depending on the style manual used):

(1) IVERSEN, GUDMUND R. and NORPOTH, HELMUT (1976) "Analysis of Variance." Sage University Paper series on Quantitative Applications in the Social Sciences, 07-001. Beverly Hills and London: Sage Pubns.

OR

(2) Iversen, Gudmund R. and Norpoth, Helmut. 1976. *Analysis of Variance.* Sage University Paper series on Quantitative Applications in the Social Sciences, series no. 07-001. Beverly Hills and London: Sage Publications.

CONTENTS

Editor's Introduction

EXPLORATORY DATA ANALYSIS (EDA) by Frederick Hartwig with Brian E. Dearing presents a set of techniques which almost every data analyst should find relevant. The questions posed in this paper and the techniques presented to deal with them are those that all data analysts must face as they begin any analysis. Application of EDA techniques will largely determine the types of other techniques which a data analyst can use to examine a given set of data. Since most EDA techniques are elementary, the reader will need little or no formal preparation in mathematics or statistics before undertaking this volume. Some knowledge of measures of central tendency and dispersion as well as some experience with elementary regression techniques might prove useful, however, to the potential reader.

The EDA techniques are appropriate for both qualitative and quantitative data as employed in bivariate and multivariate analyses in the social sciences. The emphasis of EDA is upon using visual displays to reveal vital information about the data being examined. The basic philosophy underlying the techniques is one of searching, with stress placed upon the use of alternative techniques to assess the same body of data. Hartwig and Dearing argue that a researcher should learn as much as possible about a variable or set of variables before using the data to test theories of social science relationships. If researchers know as much as possible about their data on the basis of employing EDA, the subsequent data analyses are likely to be sounder than if the researchers did not use EDA techniques. The authors' expectation is that social science data analyses will be improved through the use of EDA techniques.

In their discussion of EDA, the authors devote considerable attention to the bread-and-butter techniques for examining univariate distributions of data and bivariate relationships between variables. For univariate distributions these techniques are called the "stem and leaf" display and the "box and whisker" plot. Developed by Tukey,* these two visual techniques can yield valuable information about the shape of a distribution. An example involving a measure of interparty competition in the American states is employed to illustrate the utility of these two techniques. The authors then use the two techniques to present

*See John W. Tukey, *Exploratory Data Analysis* (Reading, MA: Addison-Wesley, 1977).

examples of typical problems associated with data distributions such as skewness, outliers, gaps, and multiple peaks.

After their discussion of univariate EDA techniques, the authors proceed to consider the techniques for examining relationships between two variables. They present the scatter plot as the technique for display of a two-variable relationship and offer the Tukey line as a method for summarizing a two-variable relationship. They then demonstrate how to "smooth" data to diminish the amount of "rough" in a relationship, thus giving the researcher a better understanding of the relationship between two variables. After illustrating how data can be smoothed, they present the "residual plot" technique as a method for examining residuals. Throughout these discussions, illustrations of the various techniques are given using socioeconomic and political data from the American states.

Once elementary EDA techniques have been used to examine the shape of a distribution or the relationship between two variables, more advanced techniques are available to "reexpress" data to overcome problems identified by the elementary techniques. The authors argue for the importance of reexpression in data analysis and present several mathematical functions which can be used to reexpress interval data. They show how reexpression can be performed with a variety of non-linear monotonic and nonmonotonic functions and illustrate persuasively the value of reexpressing data.

The paper concludes, then, with a discussion of how the EDA perspective can be used in multivariate analysis. The authors illustrate their points by employing the residual plot technique to decide which additional variables should be added at what step in a multiple regression analysis. For the reader who is unfamiliar with some of the terms used in the paper, the authors have included a glossary in which they define the major terms of EDA.

The EDA perspective outlined by the authors can be employed appropriately in all of the social science disciplines. The examples demonstrate potential uses in political science. In addition,

- The sociologist might find it appropriate to use EDA techniques before attempting to specify complex models of social behavior.
- The psychologist might find applications for these techniques in studies of attitude formation and change.
- The economist might employ them fruitfully before testing econometric models of either micro- or macroeconomic behavior. ·
- The historian might find EDA techniques useful to develop indicators of historical change.

In essence, almost every data analyst can find the EDA perspective helpful in resolving data analysis problems. And certainly before social science researchers give serious thought to undertaking a confirmatory data analysis, they should be thoroughly knowledgeable about the techniques described in EXPLORATORY DATA ANALYSIS.

—Ronald E. Weber, Editorial Board

1. THE EXPLORATORY PERSPECTIVE

Exploratory data analysis is a state of mind, a way of thinking about data analysis—and also a way of doing it. Certain techniques facilitate the exploration of data, but their use alone does not make one an exploratory data analyst. Instead, it requires a certain approach to the analysis of data, a certain perspective.

The underlying assumption of the exploratory approach is that the more one knows about the data, the more effectively data can be used to develop, test, and refine theory. Thus, the explanatory approach to data analysis seeks to maximize what is learned from the data, and this requires adherence to two principles: *skepticism* and *openness*. One should be skeptical of measures which summarize data since they can sometimes conceal or even misrepresent what may be the most informative aspects of the data, and one should be open to unanticipated patterns in the data since they can be the most revealing outcomes of the analysis. Unfortunately, data analysis in the social sciences frequently proceeds without openness, but instead with a marked unawareness of alternative patterns that might characterize the data; and it often proceeds without sufficient skepticism, placing too much trust in numerical summaries of the data.

At least part of this problem can be attributed to the false equation of data analysis with *statistics*. Although "data analysis" means the breakdown of data into its important component parts, it has been taken to mean the analysis of data by means of statistics alone, i.e., by numerical summaries of the data to the exclusion of other methods of analysis.

This ill-informed notion has two equally severe consequences. First, it tends to downgrade the importance of visual displays of data, something that is quite heavily stressed in exploratory data analysis. Instead, it leads to the belief that a statistic (such as a mean or regression coefficient) is "harder" or more "solid" than a graphical representation of data. Yet, there ought to be a healthy statistical skepticism, an awareness that even widely used statistical techniques may have unreasonable hidden assumptions about the nature of the data at hand. In fact, because numerical summaries can sometimes obscure or ignore vital information bearing upon the appropriateness of a statistic, visual analysis should precede statistical analysis even when the latter is the desired end product.

The second problem attendant to the false equation of data analysis with statistics is the *confirmatory mode* of much statistical analysis. Most of the time, statistical analysis is designed to answer questions such as: "Do the data I have confirm the hypothesis that income is related to the level of welfare expenditures in the United States?" In this confirmatory model of analysis, a model of the relationship (often linear) is fitted to the data, statistical summaries (such as means or explained variances) are obtained, and these are tested against the probability that values as high as those obtained could have occurred by chance. Not only does this mode of analysis place too much trust in statistical summaries but it also lacks openness since only two alternatives are considered. The data are not explored to see what other patterns might exist.

An alternative approach is to ask a different question: "What can these data tell me about the relationship between income and welfare expenditures in the United States?" In contrast to the confirmatory mode, this *exploratory mode* of analysis is open to a wide range of alternative explanations. This includes randomness, and it can certainly include alternatives dictated by theoretical expectations.

This is not to say that confirmatory analysis has no place in social science data analysis, but that it should not be relied upon exclusively. Though often appropriate, the exclusive use of confirmatory analysis can lead to its application when other modes of analysis might yield greater insights. The researcher should remain open to possibilities that he or she does not expect to find, particularly in the case of weak theories which do not specify models for the relationship between variables, but only that they are related to each other.

To describe the implications of the principles of skepticism and openness, the idea of data analysis needs to be explained using the most fundamental concepts in the exploratory approach:

$$\text{data} = \text{smooth} + \text{rough}.$$

The *smooth* is the underlying, simplified structure of a set of observations. It may be represented by a straight line describing the relationship between two variables or by a curve describing the distribution of a single variable, but in either case the smooth is an important feature of the data. It is the general shape of a distribution or the general shape of a relationship. It is the regularity or pattern in the data.

Since the data will almost never conform exactly to the smooth, the smooth must be extracted from the data. What is left behind is the *rough*, the deviations from the smooth, the difference between the smooth and the observed data points. What is desirable is a rough that has no smooth; that is, the rough should contain no additional pattern or structure. If the rough does contain additional structure not removed by the smooth, it is not rough enough and further smoothing should take place.

Traditionally, social science data analysis has concentrated on the smooth. The rough is not treated either as an aid in generating the smooth (is the rough rough enough?) or as a component of the data in its own right (why do these data points not fit the model?). However, the rough is just as important as the smooth, first, because smoothing is sometimes an iterative process proceeding through the examination of successive roughs for additional smooth and, second, because points that do not fit a model are often as instructive as those that do.

All data analysis is basically the partitioning of data into the smooth and the rough. Statistical techniques for obtaining explained and unexplained variances, between-group and within-group sums of squares, observed and expected cell frequencies, and so on are examples of this basic process. What distinguishes exploratory data analysis from confirmatory data analysis is the willingness to examine the rough for additional smooth and the openness to alternative models of relationships which will remove additional smooth from the rough until it is rough enough.

The principle of openness takes two interrelated forms when extracting the smooth from the rough. First, instead of imposing a hypothesized model of the smooth *on* the data, a model of the smooth is generated *from* the data. In other words, the data are explored to discover the smooth, and models generated from the data can then be compared to models specified by the theory. The more similar they are, the more the data confirm the theory.

For example, when looking at the relationship between two variables, the researcher ought not simply fit a linear model to the data, look at a summary statistic which compares the amount of rough to the amount of smooth, and then test the statistical significance of the statistic to see if the ratio could have occurred by chance. The statistic might be significant, but the relationship in the data might not be linear, i.e., the smooth might not form a straight line, or anything like it. Or the statistic might not be significant *because* the smooth is not a straight line. In either case, the researcher would have failed to discover something important about the data, namely, that the relationship between the two variables is not what he or she thought it was. Only by exploring the data is it possible to discover what is not expected, a nonlinear relationship in this case, and only by exploring the data is it possible to test fully a theory that specifies a relationship of a particular form. This can only be done by looking at the data to see what type of relationship is there and then comparing it to the theoretical expectation. In short, one should be open to alternative models of relationships between variables.

The second form that openness takes is *reexpression*. The scale on which a variable was originally observed and recorded is not the only one on which it can be expressed, and, in fact, reexpressing the original values in terms of a different scale of measurement may prove to be more workable. For example, governmental expenditure data may be originally expressed in terms of dollars, but by taking the logs of the dollar amounts, that is, reexpressing the expenditures in terms of log dollars, it may be possible to extract additional smooth from the data, i.e., discover better models of relationships involving governmental expenditures.

Because reexpression is one of the primary means by which data can be explored for unanticipated patterns, the most useful approach is to treat scales of measurement as arbitrary. Data can then be reexpressed by any transformation so long as patterns that are discovered can be related back to the original data.

The principle of skepticism also takes two forms when extracting the smooth from the data: first, a reliance on visual representations of data and, second, the use of resistant statistics.

Because of skepticism toward statistical summaries of data, major emphasis in the exploratory approach is placed on visual representations of data, and there are several graphical techniques available, both for looking at individual variables and at relationships between variables. Each has strengths and limitations, but in concert they are the data analyst's most powerful tools.

When statistical summaries are used, the exploratory approach relies more heavily than other approaches on what are called resistant statistics. Because they are more sensitive to the bulk of the data than are nonresistant statistics, they are less affected by a few highly deviant cases. As a result, they can do a better job of describing the smooth and, having done this, they make it possible to identify the rough more clearly. In contrast, nonresistant statistics can, under some conditions, blur the distinction between the smooth and the rough making it more difficult to identify both the general tendency and the deivant cases.

When applied to data analysis, the openness and skepticism principles imply a flexible, data-centered approach which is open to alternative models of relationships and alternative scales for expressing variables and which emphasizes visual representations of data and resistant statistics. The remainder of this volume explains the implementation of these ideas in the social science research environment.

Some of the terms in this book will doubtless be unfamiliar to the reader. Some are new terms for new concepts or new techniques, while others are simply new terms for old ideas. Though it might be argued that cases of the latter cause needless confusion, exploratory data analysis is a state of mind, and the new vocabulary serves the vital purpose of emphasizing the fundamental diference between exploratory data analysis and more traditional approaches. Old terms tend to perpetuate old ways of thinking, while new terms may foster new patterns of thought. The glossary of terms at the end of the book should assist the reader in becoming familiar with the vocabulary of exploratory data analysis and should help those who find themselves momentarily lost in the new terminology.

2. LOOKING AT DATA: DISTRIBUTIONS OF SINGLE VARIABLES

INTRODUCTION

A variable is a set of values each of which represents the observed value for the same characteristic for one of the cases being used in the research, as for example, expenditures per pupil for public elementary and secondary education in the United States. When these observed values are taken together and ranked from the lowest to the highest, they form what is called a distribution. In other words, the cases are distributed across a certain range of values.

The resulting distribution can be described in terms of three important characteristics: *location, spread,* and *shape.* "Location" refers to the point at which the distribution is anchored, or located, on a continuum from the lowest to the highest possible value. Where, for example, was the distribution of expenditures per pupil located in 1975? At $500? $1000? $2000? To be effective, measures of location should identify the value most characteristic of a set of cases, the one value which best describes the entire set of values, or, in other words, the value around which the other values are distributed. The location of a distribution is often measured by the mean, median, or mode. The "spread" of the distribution refers to the variability or dispersion of cases, how wide the distribution is, how spread out the cases are. This, too, is described by a single value, often the standard deviation. "Shape" is a bit more complicated, referring to the type of distribution, whether it is a bell-shaped normal distribution, symmetrical and single-peaked, whether it is skewed either to the right or the left, or multipeaked, whether it has outliers at the extremes or gaps within the distribution of values, and so on.

The standard of comparison for distributions is the bell-shaped normal curve shown in Figure 1. It is symmetrical and smooth with tails of equal length formed by a particular rate at which the number of cases declines as one moves away from the middle of the distribution in each direction. Thus, a specific percentage of cases in a normal distribution lie within one standard deviation above and below the mean (68.26%) and within two standard deviations (95.46%) and so on. Moreover, the mean (or average value) is the same as the median (the value above which and below which half of the cases lie), and these are also the same as the mode (that value which occurs most frequently). Thus, all three measures of location are the same, and they lie exactly in the middle of the distribution.

Even if all variables were normally distributed, they would still differ from one another in terms of the location of the distribution and the magnitude of the spread. The location and spread of the age distribution of a population, for example, would be greater than the comparable values for the years of formal education, even of the same population. Unfortunately, not all variables are normally distributed, and in some data sets, such as the Taylor and Hudson *World Handbook of Social and Political Indicators* (1972), one is hard-pressed to find variables with distributions that even approximate normality. As a result, variables differ from one another in terms of all three characteristics (location, spread, and shape), and identifying and describing each of these characteristics of the variables to be included in the analysis is an important step in becoming familiar with the data to be analyzed.

To do so, numerous techniques are available. They differ in a wide variety of ways, but two kinds of differences are unusually important: the extent to which they utilize *visual* representation, as opposed to purely *numeric* representation, and the extent to which they *display* the observed values, as opposed to *summarizing* the data. Combining these two distinctions creates four categories: numeric displays, numeric summaries, visual displays, and visual summaries. The techniques that have traditionally been used most often are numeric summaries, such as the mean and standard deviation, but the exploratory approach to data analysis instead makes extensive use of visual displays. The reasons for

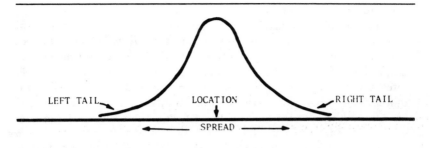

LEFT TAIL   LOCATION   RIGHT TAIL

SPREAD

Figure 1

this can be briefly stated in terms of three major tenets of the exploratory approach.

(1) The shape of a distribution is at least as important as the location and spread.

(2) Visual representations are superior to purely numeric representations for discovering the characteristic shape of a distribution.

(3) The choice of summary statistics to describe the data for a single variable should be dependent upon the appropriateness of the statistics for the shape of the distribution.

These points will be discussed one at a time.

If one is interested in economic development, the location and spread of the gross national product per capita for the nations of the world are not unimportant. However, it is at least as important to know the shape of the distribution, that it is not normal, or even symmetrical. There are many more poor nations than rich ones, and failure to realize this is to miss what is probably the most important point. In other words, location and spread are important characteristics of a distribution, but so is the shape; and because distributions with the same location and spread can have different shapes, exclusive reliance on measures of location and spread in order to describe variables can hide important differences in the way they are distributed.

The characteristic shape of distributions can be described in terms of numeric representations, but the resulting equations are sufficiently complex that few people can visualize the shapes they describe. For example, most people cannot readily perceive the shape of a normal distribution from an equation for it, whereas they can from the visual representation in Figure 1. "Shape" is a physical characteristic best communicated by visual techniques.

As for the third point, location and spread are concepts just as wealth, intelligence, alienation, and status are concepts; and like these substantive concepts, the operational indicators by which location and spread are measured are not always valid. To take two parallel examples, Stanford-Benet IQ scores are not always accurate indicators of intelligence, and means are not always accurate measures of the location of a distribution of values. Indeed, the validity of an IQ score depends in part upon the cultural bias of the test, and the validity of the mean depends in part upon the shape of the distribution. In fact, the analogy can be carried further. Some IQ tests are more culture-free than others, and some measures of location are more distribution-free than others. Because certain measures of location and spread are not valid for all distributions, the shape of a distribution should be examined before measures of location and spread are chosen; and when distributions depart markedly from the normal distribution, the more distribution-free measures are to be preferred.

It should be remembered that numeric summaries are just that; they *summarize* characteristics of distributions. Thus, the analysis should begin with the data, not with summaries of the data; and when summary statistics are used, they should accurately describe the data. Unfortunately, much data analysis in the social sciences relies entirely too much on computer-generated summary statistics while ignoring the data that are being summarized.

The conclusion which follows from these three points is that it is critically important *to look at* the shape of a distribution before choosing statistics to describe any of the characteristics of the variables to be included in the analysis. Fortunately, two relatively simple techniques for visually presenting data have been developed, both of which are described in this section along with other techniques.

Displaying Data: The Stem-and-Leaf

One of the most simple ways of displaying data is to arrange and list the observed values in either ascending or descending order. Such rank-ordered lists are useful devices since they retain all of the observed values while still providing organization to the data. However, such purely numeric displays provide little sense of the *distance* between the observed values and, therefore, little sense of the *shape* of the distribution. What is needed is the addition to the rank-ordered list of the kind of visual representation provided by the histogram. In fact, cross-breeding the two results in the *stem-and-leaf* display developed by Tukey and described in his book *Exploratory Data Analysis* (1977, ch. 1). The

```
0 | 95
1 | 19 27 55 77
2 | 00 10 64
3 | 34 36 54 79
4 | 01 06 11 13 19 30 33 36 37 38 47 49 50 51 52 53 55 61 65 66 71 80 82 84 85 86 87 88 89 94 95 96 98
5 | 00 00 00 00 04
```

Figure 2

stem-and-leaf retains all of the observed values in rank order, but it also conveys well the shape of the distribution, as Figure 2 shows.

The data in Figure 2 are based on the Index of Interparty Competition developed by Pfeiffer for the 50 United States (1967). To create the stem-and-leaf in this display, each observed value was separated into its first digit and the remaining two digits. The first digits have been listed vertically in descending order on the left and a vertical line known as the stem has been drawn just to the right of these numbers. The remaining two digits for each value have been placed in the same row as the first digit with which they belong, thus creating the leaves. Because the number of values is crucial, whenever two or more cases have the same observed value, the value for *each* case is recorded. This was done for all four states with indices of 50.0. The result is a histogram that retains and rank orders all of the observed values, losing none of the data, while still providing a picture of the shape of the distribution.

Stem-and-leaf displays using *rounded* numbers are often more useful for looking at distributions, particularly when the observed values have many digits. To create a simplified stem-and-leaf, the observed values are rounded to two digits. The second digit is recorded to the right of the stem in the row corresponding to the first digit, as shown in Figure 3.

In addition to simplifying stem-and-leaf displays, they can be stretched or condensed either by subdividing each row into two or more divisions or by combining two or more adjacent rows. The stem-and-leaf in Figure 2 is already rather condensed; over half of the cases are packed into a single row. To stretch it, each row has been subdivided into two rows: a "*" row which inclues all second digits from zero through four, and a "·" row which includes all second digits from five through nine. The resulting simplified and stretched stem-and-leaf is shown in Figure 3.

Stem-and-leaf displays can be stretched even more. For example, each row can be subdivided into five divisions: a "*" row containing all second digits of zero and one, a "t" row for all second digits of two and three, an "f" row for all fours and fives, an "s" row for all sixes and sevens, and a "·" row for all eights and nines. However, there is no

GA,MS,SC	1*	023
LA,AR	1·	68
TX,AL	2*	01
FL	2·	6
VA,NC	3*	34
TN,VT	3·	58
	4*	0111233444
	4·	55555566777888999999
	5*	00000000

Figure 3

"right" number of rows in a stem-and-leaf display. The fewer the number of rows, the more the smooth in the distribution is emphasized; the larger the number of rows, the more the rough is emphasized. Nonetheless, too few rows may crowd the data too much, obscuring the rough, while too many may spread the values too much, obscuring the smooth. The stem-and-leaf in Figure 3 is acceptable. It neither provides too much crowding nor too much detail. It strikes a balance which shows both the smooth and the rough in the distribution, and the identification of individual cases which lie in the tail(s) can be added to provide potentially helpful information.

The stem-and-leaf makes two improvements over the histogram. First, and more important, it is easier to construct by hand. In fact, it is easier to make stem-and-leaf displays than to describe how to make them, and the ease with which they are made is not unimportant. The easier it is to do something, the more likely one is to do it. In this case, it encourages the initial exploration of data. Second, the stem-and-leaf can be examined in more detail than the histogram because the bars of a histogram can hide distances between points within them. However, gaps such as these can be detected in stem-and-leaf displays because they retain the numeric values of the data. For example, the 5 and the 8 values in the 3· row in Figure 3 are farther apart than the 3 and 4 in the 3* row. Both the histogram and stem-and-leaf displays are to some degree simplifications of distributions, but the numeric values in the stem-and-leaf reduce the possibility of *over*simplification.

There is a word of warning in the use of stem-and-leaf displays. The vertical scale is dictated in part by the number system, rather than by dividing the range between the highest and lowest values by the desired number of rows. The use of the number system is what makes the stem-

and-leaf easy to construct by hand, but it can lead to inadvertently inappropriate comparisons. Displays with the same vertical scale can be compared, but as a general rule, detailed comparisons of displays should be made only when the vertical scales are equal, especially if the distributions have the same basic shape. For example, it is difficult to tell the relative height of two distributions when they have different vertical scales. In short, the stem is just as important as the leaves.

Summarizing Data

RESISTANT STATISTICS AND NUMBER SUMMARIES

To identify and describe in summary form the major characteristics of distributions, the exploratory approach to data analysis differs in three ways from the more traditional approaches. First, it relies more heavily on measures of location and spread that have the property of *resistance*. Because such statistics are less sensitive to departures from the normal distribution, they are suitable indicators of location and spread for a wider variety of distributions. Second, the approach utilizes *several* summary statistics, rather than just one or two, in order to summarize information about the shape as well as the location and spread of a distribution. Third, the exploratory approach makes use of *visual* summaries, and it does so for the same reasons that visual displays are preferred to purely numeric displays.

A resistant measure of either location or spread is one that is relatively unaffected by or resistant to changes, no matter how large, in a small proportion of the total number of cases. Because statistics which lack resistance can be sensitive to a small number of values within a disribution, usually in the tails of the distribution where there are few cases, they may not accurately describe the bulk of the cases in the middle of the distribution. For example, the mean and standard deviation, the latter in particular, are nonresistant summaries of location and spread. If the observed values formed the set [1,2,2,3,3,3,4,4,4,5,5,6], the mean would be 3.5 and the standard deviation, 1.46. However, had the highest value been 60 instead of 6, the mean would have been 8.0 and the standard deviation, 16.42. Changing just one of the 12 values produces measures of location and spread that in no way describe 11 of the 12 values in the distribution. The standard deviation is over twice as large as the entire range of these 11 values, and the mean is larger than any of them. It neither describes a typical, representative value nor does it describe a point around which most of the values in the distribution lie.

The standard deviation is a particularly nonresistant statistic and, in fact, is highly sensitive to a few extreme values. While the mean doubled in the example above, the standard deviation increased more than 11 times.

The standard deviation is the square root of the variance, and the variance is the average of the *squared* deviations from the mean:

$$\text{variance} = s_Y^2 = \left[\sum_{i=1}^{N} (Y_i - \bar{Y})^2 \right] / N.$$

The mean of the distribution ($\bar{Y}$) is subtracted from each value in the distribution (Y_i). This produces the set of *deviations from the mean* or, in other words, the distance each value lies above or below the mean. These deviations from the mean are the ($Y_i - \bar{Y}$) values in the equation. The deviations from the mean are each squared and the squares added together to produce the sum of the squared deviations from the mean, usually referred to as just the *sum of squares*. The sum of squares is then divided by the number of values in the distribution (N), producing the average of the squared deviations from the mean, which is known as the *variance*, the square root of which is the standard deviation.

What makes the standard deviation so nonresistant is the fact that the deviations from the mean are squared. As a result, cases farther and farther from the mean not only increase the sum of squares (and, therefore, the variance and standard deviation) but they also do so *at an increasing rate*. This means the sum of squares, variance, and standard deviation all have a high degree of sensitivity to extreme values, and because of this they can be unduly influenced by a small proportion of the total number of cases and fail to summarize with any accuracy the vast majority of cases.

The mean is also not resistant to an extreme value such as the one in the preceding example. However, if there is more than one such value, the extremes need to be concentrated in one tail of the distribution in order to distort the mean as a measure of location. Moreover, when this is the case, the mean is still not as sensitive to the extreme values as the standard deviation is because it does not include a square term. The mean can be a poor representative of a set of values, but not so likely and not so poor as the measure of spread provided by the standard deviation.

Several other measures more resistant than the mean and standard deviation have been developed for location (e.g., the trimmed-mean, the Winsorized-mean, and the biweight) and for spread (e.g., the median absolute deviation or MAD; see Gross, 1976; Huber, 1972; Lax, 1975; and Mosteller and Tukey, 1977). While each of these has certain virtues, among the most simple and most useful resistant measures are the *order* statistics, so called because they are based upon the rank order of the values in a distribution. The median, for example, is that value above which and below which fall one-half of the values in a rank-ordered list. It is either the middle value in a rank-ordered list with an odd number of cases or the point midway between the two middle values in a rank-ordered list with an even number of cases. The lower *hinge* is that point above which three-fourths and below which one-fourth of the values lie (the bottom quartile), and the upper hinge is that point above which lie one-fourth of the values (the top quartile) and below which lie the other three-fourths. The distance between the lower hinge and the upper hinge is sometimes referred to by the imposing name "interquartile range," but *midspread* is both easier and more descriptive.

The resistant nature of the median and midspread can be illustrated by the earlier example. With the values ranging from 1 through 6, the median is 3.5, the same as the mean. However, replacing the 6 with 60 does not change the median at all; it remains 3.5 since this is still the middle value in the distribution. Likewise, the midspread is a resistant measure of spread. In the first distribution, the lower and upper hinges are 2.5 and 4.5, and the midespread, 2.0. Because replacement of the 6 with 60 does not alter the two hinges, the midspread remains 2.0 in the second distribution.

This is not to say the median and midspread remain the same no matter how many values in a distribution are changed, as the above example might imply. They are, however, highly resistant to changes in the extreme values, i.e., in the shape of the tails of a distribution. As a result, they provide values which represent well the typical value in a distribution and the spread of the other values around it even when the tails of a distribution depart markedly from the shape they assume in a normal distribution.

A resistant summary of some of the major features of a distribution can be created by combining the median and hinges with the highest and lowest values. This produces a five-number summary, which looks like this for the Index of Interparty Competition:

9.50	40.10	45.05	48.60	50.40

Here 9.50 is the lowest value; 40.10 is the lower hinge; 45.05, the median; 48.60, the upper hinge; and 50.40, the highest value. As with the rank-ordered list, the five-number summary provides little sense of distance, although this can be partially corrected by adding the numeric representation of the distances between adjacent values:

9.50		40.10		45.05		48.60		50.40
	30.60		4.95		3.55		1.80	

And this can be further elaborated by finding the numeric distances between the median and the lowest and highest values and the distance between the lower and upper hinges.

9.50		40.10		45.05		48.60		50.40
	30.60		4.95		3.55		1.80	
		35.55		8.50		5.35		

The values in the bottom row are "half-ranges." In contrast to the full range of the data between the highest and lowest values, each of these values describes the range of one-half of the data points. The one on the left describes the range of the lower half of the data, hence the name *lowspread*. The middle of the three describes the range of that half of the data which falls in the middle of the distribution, hence the name *midspread*. The one on the right describes the range of the highest one-half of the data points, hence the name *highspread*.

Number summaries lack detail, but they still provide information about all three characteristics of a distribution. The median indicates the location of the distribution; the midspread is a measure of spread; and a comparison of the distances can provide information about the shape. For variables with a bell-shaped normal distribution, or something approximating it, the symmetrical nature of the distribution would be indicated by approximate equality between three pairs of values: (1) the lowspread and the highspread, (2) the distances between the median and each of the hinges, and (3) the distances between each of the hinges and the extremes. Moreover, the distances between the median and each of the hinges would be less than the distances between the hinges and the extremes because of the greater number of cases in the middle of the distribution compared to the tails.

Obviously, the Index of Interparty Competition does not conform to this picture. The distance between the lower hinge and the lowest value is 17 times the distance between the upper hinge and the highest value (30.60 compared with 1.80), and the lowspread of 35.55 is nearly 7 times that of the highspread of 5.35. Thus, the number summary indicates the same abnormality in the distribution that is revealed by the stem-and-leaf, although the lack of detail in the summary obscures the reason for it —a series of extreme values in the left tail of the distribution.

THE BOX-AND-WHISKER

As useful as the number summary is, numeric representations of distances are not as effective as visual representations. Thus, by adding visual representation to the number summary, perception of the major characteristics of distributions can be greatly facilitated. The *box-and-whisker* plot, also developed by Tukey (1977), does precisely this; and moreover, the box-and-whisker provides detail when it is often needed most, whenever one or both of the tails of a distribution contain extremely large or small values.

A box-and-whisker for the Index of Interparty Competition is shown in Figure 4. The vertical line forming the left side of the box is located at the lower hinge; the right-hand side of the box is located at the upper hinge; and the vertical line within the box represents the location of the median value in the distribution. Thus, half of all cases in the distribution lie within the box, with one-fourth of the cases between the median and one side of the box and another fourth between the median and the other side.

The "X's" mark the cases farthest from but still within one midspread of the two hinges, and these are connected to the box with dashed lines known as whiskers. Any cases beyond this are marked individually, with

Figure 4

cases more than 1.5 midspreads from the hinges marked with darkened circles.

Because almost exactly 2.5% of all cases in a *normal* distribution lie below the point defined by the lower hinge minus one midspread and another 2.5% lie above the upper hinge plus one midspread, 95% of all cases in a normal distribution will lie within the range defined by the endpoints of the whiskers. Thus, a distribution with much more than 5% of the values outside this range, i.e., individually marked, begins to depart from normality and can be rather quickly identified.

By comparing the box-and-whisker in Figure 4 with the number summary presented earlier for the same Index of Interparty Competition data, it can be seen that distances represented numerically in the number summary are more effectively communicated by the box-and-whisker because of its visual nature. Moreover, the detail provided by the box-and-whisker for the left tail of the distribution shows the reason for the greater lowspread compared to the highspread, namely, the eight extreme values on the low end of the distribution.

The box-and-whisker can also be compared to the stem-and-leaf for the same data, shown earlier in Figure 3, by mentally turning the stem-and-leaf a quarter turn counterclockwise. The eight extreme values on the left side of the box-and-whisker appear as the cases ranging from 10 to 26 in the stem-and-leaf. The longer whisker on the left matches the more gradual decline from the peak shown in the stem-and-leaf, due in large part to the four cases in the 3* and 3: rows, and the slightly off-center median within the box is the result of the greater number of cases in the 4: row than the 4* row.

There is as yet no set of conventions governing the design of box-and-whisker plots. McNeil (1977) recommends the use of 1.0 and 1.5 midspreads above and below the hinges as the criteria for marking individual cases with light and dark circles, while Tukey (1977) recommends the use of 1.5 and 3.0 midspreads. There is also variation in marking the median. Sometimes a vertical line is used; sometimes an asterisk is used; and sometimes the box is notched to indicate the location of the median. Moreover, when parallel box-and-whiskers are being used to summarize and compare distributions with unequal numbers of cases, the height of the box can be varied (or the width if they are arranged vertically) to represent the larger number of cases in some distributions than in others (McGill et al., 1978).

There is also variation in which pair of values is used to anchor the box-and-whisker. In this text, the highest and lowest values have been used in order to have plots of equal length. When this is done, the numeric distance between the two extreme values is divided by the number of spaces on the continuum, and each space comes to represent a certain numeric distance. For example, the range for the Index of Interparty Competition is 40.90. Each of the 60 spaces (a convenient number of spaces on a typewriter) is equal to 40.90/60, or .68. Therefore, the number of spaces from the lowest value (9.50) to the lower hinge (40.90) is (40.90 - 9.50)/.68, or 45 spaces. Likewise, the distance between the upper hinge and the highest value is equal to 1.80/.68, which rounds to 3 spaces, and the distance between the median and the highest value is 5.35/.68, or 8 spaces.

An alternative particularly useful when comparing the distributions of different variables is to anchor the box-and-whisker plots at the hinges. This is done by locating the hinges at specific points on the continuum, say 20 and 40, dividing the midspread by the distance between two points, then using the quotient to mark off the median, the whiskers, and any individual values beyond the whiskers. When this is done, the boxes are all the same width and located at the same place on the continuum, thereby making differences in the location both of medians and values beyond the whiskers especially noticeable. The plots may not all nicely fit on a page, but differences in the shape of the distributions being compared will be readily apparent.

Because they do not specify each of the observed values, box-and-whisker plots are visual summaries rather than displays. They do not show everything that stem-and-leaf displays show, but they do provide a better picture of the tails of a distribution. Therefore, box-and-whisker plots are particularly valuable for identifying and communicating the major characteristics of distributions whose tails deviate from those of the normal distribution.

UNDERSTANDING DATA

The techniques just described are an important part of the exploratory approach to data analysis, but they are only means by which to look at data. In order to understand the data to be used in research, it is necessary not only to know how to look *at* the data but also to know what to look for *in* the data.

Four different characteristics stand out as unusually important: (1) skewness, (2) outliers, (3) gaps, and (4) multiple peaks. These will be discussed and illustrated with examples using the techniques just described: stem-and-leaf displays, resistant statistics, and box-and-whisker plots.

Skewness

Skewed distributions often resemble symmetrical distributions with one whole side of the distribution pulled outward. This not only results in a string of extreme values on one side of the distribution but also results in a median that is off-center with respect to the hinges and a box formed by the hinges that is off-center with respect to the highest and lowest values. Because of this, the extreme values on one side of the distribution are not separate from the rest of the distribution, but instead are an extension of it.

A good example of skewness is provided by the Index of Interparty Competition that has been used as an example throughout this section. The skewness shows up in the stem-and-leaf display in Figure 3, the box-and-whisker in Figure 4, and in the number summary as well. Even a cursory examination of the table of indices provided in the Pfeiffer article reveals the skewness. Most of the states have competitive party systems since the "Two-Party" category includes 28 of the 50 states and an additional 10 states have "Weak Two—Party" systems. In contrast, only 12 states have "One-Party" or "Modified One-Party" systems. In short, fewer states have noncompetitive party systems than competitive ones, and this asymmetry suggests skewness in the distribution.

That the entire distribution is skewed is shown by the number summary, in which the range of the first quartile (30.60) exceeded that of the second quartile (4.95), which exceeded that of the third quartile (3.55), which exceeded that of the highest quartile (1.80). As a result, the low-spread of 35.55 was greater than the midspread of 8.50, and this was greater than the highspread of 5.35. Thus, the asymmetry is not limited to a few extreme values but, rather, permeates the whole of the distribution.

Skewness in distributions presents problems for nonresistant measures of location and spread. A few extreme, "oddball" values can distort the mean and standard deviation, but the consequences of a whole string of values which are genuinely part of a skewed distribution are even more serious. For example, the mean and standard deviation for the Pfeiffer Index of Interparty Competition are 40.72 and 11.49, respectively. Only 28% of the values lie below the mean, and as shown by the stem-and-leaf in Figure 3, it is not a very typical or representative value. The vast majority of cases lie above the mean, so it is not located at a point where there are very many other values. It is neither representative nor does it define the location of the distribution, the point around which the values are distributed.

The standard deviation is also distorted by the string of extreme values. Of the Pfeiffer indices, 84% lie within one standard deviation of the mean, and, more significantly, all eight values lying beyond one standard deviation from the mean lie below it. None lies more than one standard deviation above the mean, even though the extreme values have pulled the mean too far in the opposite direction, toward the low end of the distribution.

In more substantive terms, the mean value of 40.72 suggests that party systems in the United States are less competitive than they actually are, and the standard deviation of 11.49 indicates greater variation among them than really exists. The mean and standard deviation fail to convey the fact that most states have two highly competitive political parties.

The location and spread of the distribution are better conveyed by the median of 45.05 and the midspread of 8.50, but these are not perfect either. In fact, no measures of location and spread can accurately describe the major characteristics of seriously skewed distributions. Measures of location and spread that are highly resistant better describe the bulk of the cases, but they fail to point out the large range of values from the lowest to the highest ones. On the other hand, nonresistant measures fail to convey the tight packing of cases into a narrow range at one end of the distribution. Thus, the only acceptable way to describe distributions which are severely skewed is through visual representations such as the stem-and-leaf and box-and-whisker. The dominant fact of a skewed distribution is not its location or spread but its shape, and this is best described by visual techniques.

Outliers

An outlier is a value which lies outside the normal range of the data, i.e., lies well above or well below most, or even all, of the other values in a distribution. It is difficult to say at just what point a value becomes an outlier since much depends upon its relationship to the rest of the data and the use for which the data is intended. One may want to identify and set aside outlying cases in order to concentrate on the bulk of the data,

28

but, on the other hand, it may be the outliers themselves on which the analysis should be concentrated. For example, communities with abnormally low crime rates may be the most instructive ones.

A good example of an outlier is provided by one of the variables sometimes used along with other variables to measure industrial development at the national level: the number of miles of railroad per square mile of land. This variable appears in Banks's *Cross-Polity Time-Series Data* (1971) and also in Stallings's (1972) monograph on the economic dependency of third world nations. The box-and-whisker in Figure 5 shows the distribution of this variable for the 26 Western Hemispheric nations. Obviously one case is radically different from all others, and the visual representation provided by the box-and-whisker makes this dramatically clear.

The effect of an extreme value on nonresistant summary statistics is also demonstrated by this example. The mean and standard deviation are 37.75 and 99.86, respectively. All but the outlying case fall within one standard deviation from the mean, and the mean is so large that it lies well above the upper hinge. It is hardly a typical or representative value, and the standard deviation hardly describes with much accuracy the spread of the values in the distribution. In contrast, the median and midspread values of 15.05 and 23.50 are much more representative of the data. The extreme length of the right tail caused by the outlier does not affect either measure because of its resistance with respect to the tails of a distribution.

One other point can be made with this example. The value for the outlying case, Cuba, is sufficiently different from the other values that one should suspect an error in the data, and, upon reflection, were the railroad right-of-way in Cuba a relatively narrow 10 feet, Cuba would be almost entirely covered by railroads. In such cases, an alternate source should be consulted, and the *Statistical Abstract of Latin America: 1972* reports a total railroad mileage in 1967 of 3156. Since this works out to 71.75 miles per square mile of land, a value more in line with the other data, the 518.8 figure in the Banks (and Stallings) data is

Figure 5

probably an error. However, the point is not the error itself, but (1) the necessity of examining data before using them, (2) the effectiveness of visual representations in identifying major characteristics of data, and (3) the effect of outliers on nonresistant measures of location and spread.

Gaps and Multiple Peaks

Two other characteristics to look for in data are distributions with gaps and ones that have more than the single-peak characteristic of the normal distribution. Distributions with multiple peaks also have valleys between the peaks, and together they create a distribution that looks like it is made of two or more smaller distributions. Figure 6 shows two different visual representations of the cross-national data for the percent of the population over the age of 14 that is literate (Taylor and Hudson, 1972). The cases tend to cluster at the extremes, showing the multiple-peak characteristic, and the lack of cases with values between 50 and 60 creates a gap in the distribution. In fact, the display shows two rather separate distributions: one from 2% to 50% literate and one from 60% to 100% literate. The former has right skew; the latter has a left skew; and between the two is a gap of 10%.

Multiple-peaked distributions present difficult problems for measures of location, especially bimodal (double-peaked) distributions. For example, the mean percent literature is 54.0. This is, in one sense, the middle of the distribution, but it falls in the gap between the two groups of data and, as a result, certainly does not represent a typical rate of literacy.

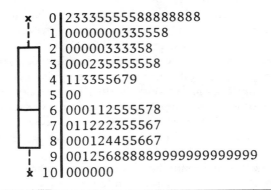

Figure 6

The median of 60.0 for the same data is not much of an improvement, if any, but then there is no one point of location, no one point around which the values are distributed. Hence, no one measure of location will prove to be very useful.

The basic problem is that multiple-peaked distributions are too complex to be summarized. Knowing that the mean rate of literacy is 54.0% and the standard deviation is 34.0% is not very informative, and it is not any more so to know that the median is 60.0% and the midspread is 65.0%. In fact, if in the absence of a visual representation one simply visualized a symmetrical, single-peaked distribution, one would assume a distribution with just the opposite shape from that which actually exists.

Notice also that the stem-and-leaf in Figure 6 is more instructive than the box-and-whisker. The excessively long box and abbreviated whiskers indicate something abnormal in the distribution, but not precisely what it is. Box-and-whisker plots provide the best picture of the tails of a distribution, but for problems lying in the middle of a distribution, the stem-and-leaf is invaluable.

Because of the difficulties inherent in working with distributions like that shown in Figure 6, it is sometimes useful to split such distributions, work with them separately, and then try to piece them together at the end. This is particularly true when there is a logical explanation for the shape of the original distribution.

Summary

There are two major points in this section. First, in order to understand a set of data, it is not enough to rely on summary statistics of location and spread, such as the mean and standard deviation. There are two reasons for this. The first is that many variables depart markedly from the shape of a normal distribution by having outliers, skewness, or multiple peaks; and whenever such abnormalities occur, the shape of a distribution, rather than its location and spread, is likely to be its most important characteristic. However, neither individually nor jointly can measures of location and spread alone describe the shape of the distribution of a variable. Thus, exclusive reliance on measures of location and spread can cause one to miss the most important characteristic of a set of observations.

The second reason for not relying exclusively on measures of location and spread is that it is impossible to tell when and how one is being misled without knowing the shape of the distribution. Thus it becomes important to look at the shape of the distribution not only to learn its shape but also to choose the most appropriate measures of the location of the distribution and the spread of values around the point of location.

The second major point in this section has been that shape is best perceived visually; and, therefore, major emphasis has been placed on two different ways of visually representing data: the stem-and-leaf and the box-and-whisker. The former is a display which retains the numeric representation of data points while arranging them into the shape of the distribution. The latter is a visual summary which provides detail at the ends of the distribution. Both are useful ways to observe the characteristic shape of the distribution of a single variable.

3. LOOKING AT DATA: RELATIONSHIPS BETWEEN VARIABLES

Introduction

For some research questions it is sufficient to know the location, spread, and shape of the distribution of each variable, but more often necessary to examine the *relationship* between two or more variables.

Like distributions of single variables, relationships between variables have three important characteristics, one of which is shape. The other two are strength and direction. The strength of a relationship refers to the extent to which data points on one variable correspond to the data points on the other variable. Often this is determined by the extent to which the observed values on one variable can be predicted from the corresponding values on the other variable. For example, the more accurately levels of interparty competition in the United States can be predicted from levels of income, the more strongly income and interparty competition are related to each other. In the terminology of the exploratory approach, strength refers to the relative importance of the smooth as compared with the rough. The closer the data points are to the smooth, the stronger is the relationship or, in other words, the less rough that remains after the smooth has been removed, the more strongly two variables are related to each other. In some sense, it is also true that the simpler the smooth is, the stronger the relationship is; that closeness to the smooth is not only important but also the simplicity of the smooth.

Direction refers to the question of whether high values on one variable are associated with high values on the other variable (and low values on one with low values on the other) or whether high values on the first variable are associated with *low* values on the second variable (and low values on the first, with *high* values on the second). The former is a positive relationship; the latter, a negative one. For example, if it were true that the higher the level of income in a state, the higher the level of interparty competition, the relationship would be positive. If, on the other hand, the higher the level of income, the *lower* the level of party competition, then the relationship would be negative.

It is possible, of course, for a single relationship to have more than one direction. A U-shaped relationship, for example, changes from a negative to a positive direction, and this leads to the third characteristic of relationships.

The shape of a relationship refers to the way in which variables are related to each other or, in other words, to the shape of the line formed by the smooth. This may be a straight line, in which case differences on one variable are always proportional to differences on the other variable, or it may be a curve, as occurs, for example, when increases on one variable are associated with increases on the other variable at an increasing rate. Or the shape of the relationship may be some kind of compound curve, such as the S-shaped ogive.

Thus, relationships can differ from each other in terms of strength, direction, and shape, and indentifying and describing these characteristics of relationships is typically the most important step in the analysis of data.

Displaying Relationships: The Scatter Plot

One way to display the data for a two-variable relationship is in numeric form by listing the observed values for one variable in rank order and then listing the observed value for each case on the other variable next to its value on the first variable. However, it is difficult to get a sense of the strength of the relationship from a display of this type, much less a sense of the shape of the relationship.

Both of these characteristics can be more easily grasped by a visual representation of the data in a display called a *scatter plot*. A display of this type is shown in Figure 7 in which the Index of Interparty Competition is plotted on the vertical axis against the median family income for each state (U.S. Bureau of the Census, 1973) on the horizontal axis. Each pair of data points, one for each of the 48 cases, is represented by a single dot located directly above the observed value on the horizontal axis (the "X" variable) and directly opposite the observed value on the vertical axis (the "Y" variable). Thus, for ex-

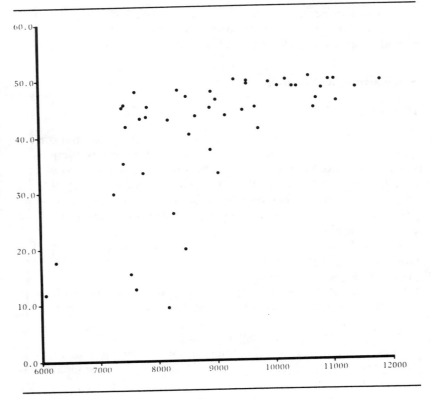

Figure 7

ample, the last case in Figure 7 is located above 11811 on the horizontal axis and opposite 49.79 on the vertical axis.

All three characteristics of relationships are evident in scatter plots. When the observed values go from the lower left-hand corner (low values on both variables) to the upper right-hand corner (high values on both variables), the scatter plot shows a positive relationship, as in Figure 7. When they go from the upper left to the lower right corner, the relationship is negative. The shape of the relationship is indicated by the line approximated by the observed values (a curved line in Figure 7), and the strength of the relationship is indicated by the extent to which the observed values conform to the line. The greater the spread around the line, the weaker the relationship. (Notice that in Figure 7 the observed values are more spread out vertically on the left side of the plot and more tightly packed on the right side.) Thus, scatter plots are among the most effective tools for data analysis because they provide such a complete picture of the relationship between variables.

Summarizing Relationships

FITTING A LINE

Scatter plots display all of the data for a relationship, but for the data analyst, the task is to break the relationship into its component parts, into the smooth and rough. This can be done by visual inspection, by simply "eyeballing" the scatter plot to see if any patterns exist, but more systematic techniques less subject to differences in individual perceptiveness and more appropriate for complex relationships are clearly desirable.

One of the more obvious things to do with a scatter plot is to fit a straight line to the relationship. Indeed, this is not only what many people do anyway, at least mentally when they "eyeball" a relationship that has some degree of linearity but also it often serves as a good "first smooth," a workable first step in the iterative process of exploring relationships.

The most common method for fitting a line to the data is least-squares linear regression. (See the appropriate chapters in Blalock, 1972; Hayes, 1973; Kmenta, 1971; or almost any other standard statistics text.) However, this is not always an appropriate method for the data at hand and, from an exploratory perspective, an alternative to the least-squares regression line, the *Tukey line*, is often more useful.

The basic problem with the least-squares regression line is that it lacks resistance. In fact, since it is based on the mean-variance combination, this is not very surprising. The least-squares regression line is located such that it minimizes the residual variance, and this means it must minimize the sum of the squared residual values. Hence the term *least-squares* regression.

Because the residual values are squared, cases lying farther and farther from the regression line increase the sum of the squared residuals at an increasing rate, and because of the least-squares criterion, i.e., the need to minimize the sum of the squared residuals, a few cases that would otherwise lie far from the regression line can exert substantial influence over the location of the line. As a result, the regression line will tend to track these cases, which is to say it will have to come reasonably close to them to satisfy the least-squares criterion and, therefore, the least-squares regression line will lack resistance to the excessive influence of a few atypical cases.

In contrast, the Tukey line is more resistant, as shown by a comparison of the regression line "R" and the Tukey line "T" in a plot (Figure 8) of the Democratic vote for President in 1952 on the vertical axis against the Democratic vote for President in 1948 (U.S. Bureau of the Census, 1954). The location of both lines is strongly influenced by the four cases in the upper left-hand corner of the scatter plot, but the Tukey line less so than the least-squares line. Neither line describes very well the relationship which exists for the bulk of the cases on the right side of the plot, but the Tukey line performs better than the least-squares line. In fact, the negative slope of the least-squares regression line is completely misleading.

The reason the Tukey line is more resistant is that its location is based on medians, which are themselves resistant, and the line is also less influenced by cases located in the tails of the distribution of either of the two variables.

As McNeil (1977) describes it, a Tukey line is fitted to the data in the following way. First, the relationship is sliced along the horizontal axis into three nonoverlapping groups with approximately one-third of the cases in each slice. Second, the median of the X values in the first slice is determined (MDX_1), as is the median of the X values in the last slice (MDX_3), the median of the Y values in the first slice (MDY_1), and the median of the Y values in the last slice (MDY_3).

If one is working directly on a scatter plot, the two cross-medians are located, i.e., the points (MDX_1, MDY_1) and (MDX_3, MDY_3) and a transparent straightedge connecting these two points is placed on the plot. The straightedge is then moved parallel to its original position until half of the cases are above and half are below the edge, and then a line is drawn, the Tukey line.

Arithmetically this can be done by determining the slope ("b") and the intercept ("a") coefficients for the following formula for a straight line: $\hat{Y}_i = a + bX_i$. The slope is equal to $(MDY_3 - MDY_1)/(MDX_3 - MDX_1)$, while the intercept is the median of the following values: $D_i = Y_i - bX_i$. The Tukey line can then be drawn on the scatter plot by a line between any two X_i, Y_i points.

The property of resistance in a line used as a smoother is desirable because it is less likely to blur the distinction between the smooth and the rough. Because the location of the line is less affected by a few deviant cases, such cases are less likely to appear as part of the smooth when they should appear as part of the rough. This is particularly important when the line is being used as the "first smooth" in an iterative process of examining both the smooth and the rough in a relationship.

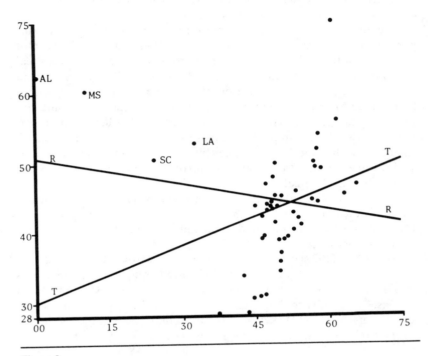

Figure 8

SMOOTHING THE DATA

Two variables are related to each other whenever the values on one variable (Y) vary systematically with the values on the other variable (X). For example, in a U-shaped relationship, the values on the Y variable decrease with increasing values on the X variable, then level off and begin to increase with still further increases in X. Whenever a relationship like this occurs, *measures of location* for the Y values will also vary systematically from one range of X to another. In the example of a U-shaped relationship, they will be high in the lowest range of X, decrease with increasing ranges of X, level off, increase, and again be high in the uppermost range of X.

What this suggests is the possible use of successive measures of location as a means for observing the smooth in a relationship and, indeed, the smooth in a relationship is the two-dimensional analogue of the point of location for the distribution of a single variable. The point of location is that point around which the values are distributed, as well as the one point which best describes the observed values. Likewise, the smooth in a relationship is the *line* around which the data points in a relationship are distributed, as well as the one line which best describes the relationship. Hence, the smooth can be thought of as a line formed by a series of points of location on Y within progressively increasing ranges of X.

Because the smooth should be resistant to the effects of unusual cases, just as the measure of location should be, medians can serve well as the measures of location for the Y values. Therefore, one of the systematic ways to represent the smooth is to determine the medians of the Y values within progressively increasing but overlapping ranges of X, or what are known as *running medians*.

This can best be shown by reference to Table 1, which displays the Democratic percentage of the total vote for President from 1896 to 1972 (Congressional Quarterly, 1975).

Running medians have to be taken for a constant number of values, five in this case. Thus, the first five values in the series are taken (46.73, 45.51, 37.60, 43.05, 41.84) and the median of these five determined (43.05) and recorded (in the column labeled "5") next to the middle of the first five values. Then, the next number in the series is included (49.24) and the first value dropped (46.73), leaving a new but overlapping group of five values (45.51, 37.60, 43.05, 41.84, 49.24). The median of these five values is then determined (also 43.05) and recorded next to the middle of these five values; the next value in the series is added to the group (34.17) and the first of the five dropped (45.51), moving the group of five values used to determine the median one number farther along in the series (now 37.60, 43.05, 41.84, 49.24, 34.17). The median of this new group is determined (41.84) and recorded next to the middle value, and so on until the last five values in the entire series are used and the median determined and recorded. The column in Table 1 containing these running medians is labeled "5" to denote the use of groups of five.

Running medians do create a problem of end values since two data points are lost at each end of the series when groups of five are used. The easiest way to handle this is to determine the next to the end values by using the medians of the first three values and the last three values and to determine the end values by simply copying on the end values from the previous series. Thus, the first value is the same in both the original series and smoothed series (46.73), as is the last value (37.53), and the second value (45.51) is the median of the first three values (46.73, 45.51,

TABLE 1
Smoothing Democratic Percentage of the Vote for
President: 1896-1972

Year	DEM%	5	3	3R'	(H)	53R'H
1896	46.73	(46.73)	(46.73)	(46.73)		46.73
1900	45.51	(45.51)	45.51	45.51	46.12	45.20
1904	37.60	43.05	43.05	43.05	44.28	43.66
1908	43.05	43.05	43.05	43.05	43.05	42.72
1912	41.84	41.84	41.84	41.84	42.44	42.14
1916	49.24	41.84	41.84	41.84	41.84	41.57
1920	34.17	40.77	40.77	40.77	41.30	41.04
1924	28.84	40.77	40.77	40.77	40.77	40.77
1928	40.77	40.77	40.77	40.77	40.77	44.26
1932	57.42	54.70	54.70	54.70	47.74	51.22
1936	60.79	54.70	54.70	54.70	54.70	54.70
1940	54.70	54.70	54.70	54.70	54.70	54.37
1944	53.39	53.39	53.59	53.59	54.04	52.74
1948	49.51	49.51	49.51	49.51	51.45	50.48
1952	44.38	49.51	49.51	49.51	49.51	49.51
1956	41.97	49.51	49.51	49.51	49.51	48.22
1960	49.72	44.38	44.38	44.38	46.94	45.24
1964	61.05	42.72	42.72	42.72	43.55	43.14
1968	42.72	(42.72)	42.72	42.72	42.72	41.42
1972	37.53	(37.53)	(37.53)	(37.53)	40.12	37.53

37.60), while the second to last value (42.72) is the median of the last three values (61.05, 42.72, 37.53).

Having taken running medians of group five, the next step is to smooth this new sequence further by taking running medians of group three. The procedure is the same, except that medians are determined for sequences of three cases instead of five. The results of this are shown in the column labeled "3" in Table 1, where the end values have just been copied on from the "5" series.

To make sure *this* sequence is as smooth as possible, the process of taking running medians of groups three is repeated until no further changes occur. This is shown in the column labeled "3R'." The "R" denotes the use of *repeated* running medians, and the prime symbol denotes the use of end values copied from the previous sequence.

The use of running medians is the primary smoothing technique, but to this is added a second one, *hanning*, named by Tukey after an "Austrian meteorologist of the last century, who liked to smooth weather information . . . in this way" (Tukey, 1977: 234). Hanning involves the repetition twice of running medians of group two, but because the median of two numbers is the point midway between them, running medians of group two are the same as averages. The sixth column in Table 1, labeled "(H)," shows the first stage. The average (46.12) of the first two 3R′ values (46.73, 45.51) is computed and recorded on the half-line. Then the next value in the 3R′ series is added (43.05) and the first one dropped (46.73), and the average (44.28) of the two values (45.51, 43.05) is computed and recorded. This procedure of running medians (or moving averages) of group two is repeated through the last two values in the 3R′ series.

The second stage is to compute running medians of group two on the values computed in the first stage. In Table 1 this results in the values from 45.20 through 41.42 in the last column; the end values are again copied from the 3R′ series to complete the sequence. This last column is labeled "53R′H" to indicate the use of running medians of group five, followed by running medians of group three, the repetition of this process until the sequence of numbers no longer changes, the use of end values copied from previous sequences, and, last of all, hanning.

This last column is a numeric representation of the smooth in the Democratic percentage of the vote for President from 1896 to 1972. However, the major characteristics of the smooth are more clearly evident in the visual respresentation shown in Figure 9. From this one can see the rise in the fortunes of the Democratic Party beginning with the candidacy of Al Smith in 1928 and reaching a peak with the landslide victory of Franklin D. Roosevelt in 1936. Also evident from the smooth is a steady decline since then, reaching a post-Depression low with the candidacy of George McGovern in 1972. Note also the resistant nature of the smooth reflected in the difference between the two largest victories for Democratic candidates: Roosevelt's in 1936 and Johnson's in 1964. The former is part of the trend. The upward slope of the smooth nearly reaches the Roosevelt percentage, while the downward trend from that point on is unaffected by the highly deviant Johnson landslide.

MEDIAN AND HINGE TRACES

One of the principles of smoothing is that whatever procedures are used to smooth one of the variables must also be applied to the other variable. In the case of time-series data, such as the Democratic vote for

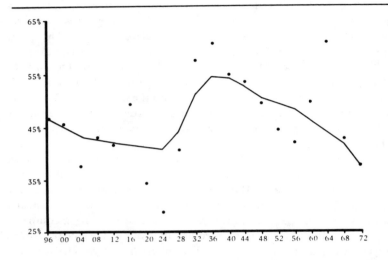

Figure 9

President, the "observed values" on the X variable (time) are equally spaced along the horizontal axis and, as a result, no amount of smoothing will alter them.

In contrast, relationships such as that between median family income and the Index of Interparty Competition almost never have equally spaced values on the horizontal axis. Therefore, smoothing procedures used on Y must also be applied to X, thus increasing the work involved. Moreover, the number of cases underlying many relationships of this type is often rather large, further contributing to the amount of time required to smooth the relationship.

Fortunately, a short cut can be taken which reduces the amount of work involved and, as a result, probably increases the likelihood that smoothing will be done. Instead of taking running medians of group five, the short cut is to *slice* the relationship like a loaf of bread along the horizontal axis and determine the median values within each slice. For example, the relationship between median family income and interparty competition can be sliced into eight nonoverlapping groups of six cases each. The first six cases on the horizontal axis (the six states with the lowest median family incomes) form the first slice; the next six cases form the second slice; and so on through the six cases with the highest values on X.

There is, of course, nothing sacred about slices of six cases each. In fact, the size of the slices should depend upon the total number of cases; the more cases, the larger the slices. Second, the size of the slices should depend upon the amount of detail desired; the larger the number of slices, the more detail that will be included. In practice, half a dozen to a dozen slices works well to summarize the relationship.

Having sliced the relationship, the median for the Y values for each set of six cases is determined and the sequence of slice medians is then smoothed by a 3R'H process. Running medians of group five are not taken first because the slice medians serve as the short cut for this first series of running medians.

Having smoothed the medians on Y, it is now necessary to determine the median values on X within each slice and smooth them by the same process. However, because they already appear in rank order, 3R' smoothing is unnecessary since it will not change any of the values.

The rough in a relationship is often as important as the smooth, so it is appropriate to examine it, too. This can be done by simply determining the upper and lower hinges within each slice and smoothing these values in the same way the medians were smoothed. The smoothed median and hinge values are shown in Table 2.

Though the medians and hinges have been smoothed numerically, it is not until they are given visual representation that they can contribute to an understanding of the relationship. This is accomplished by crossing the smoothed medians within each slice to form a series of X, Y points (7340, 32.68; 7730, 34.94; 8237, 38.63; and so on), then locating the points on a two-dimensional plot and forming the *median trace* by a line connecting the points. This forms the middle of the three lines in Figure 10.

The *hinge traces*, which appear in Figure 10 as the two outer traces, are formed in the same way, except the upper hinge on X should not always be crossed with the upper hinge on Y and the lower hinge with the lower hinge. Instead, the upper hinges should be crossed whenever the sequence of cross-hinges is rising, as should the lower hinges, and the lower hinge on X should be crossed with the *upper* hinge on Y and the upper hinge on X with the *lower* hinge on Y whenever the sequence is falling. If this is not done, the hinge traces can create the appearance of greater spread around the smooth than actually exists.

What the median and hinge traces show in Figure 10 is a relationship that is neither linear nor has a constant spread of cases throughout the range of the relationship. Instead, the relationship is curvilinear, one in which the level of party competition increases, but at a decreasing rate. The spread of cases is also noticeably greater among the lower

TABLE 2
Smoothing Slice Medians and Hinges—Median Family Income, 1970
Index of Interparty Competition

MD IPC	3R'H MD IPC	MD MFI	H MD MFI
32.68	32.68	7340	7340
37.73	34.94	7673	7730
34.66	38.63	8236	8237
44.38	43.03	8804	8774
45.62	46.08	9254	9286
48.71	47.94	9834	9858
48.74	48.84	10512	10476
49.20	49.20	11048	11048

LH IPC	3R'H LH IPC	UH IPC	3R'H UH IPC	LH MFI	H LH MFI	UH MFI	H UH MFI
17.66	17.66	45.16	45.16	6273	6273	7441	7441
15.54	18.24	43.33	45.20	7530	7375	7774	7843
19.97	24.54	45.32	45.75	8167	8107	8381	8366
40.57	36.20	47.07	47.23	8564	8586	8929	8932
43.72	43.28	49.64	48.90	9049	9090	9970	9470
45.12	45.15	49.44	49.68	9698	9690	9970	10030
46.65	46.71	50.01	49.90	10313	10321	10692	10690
48.44	48.44	49.99	49.99	10959	10959	11407	11407

Symbols: IPC = Index of Party Competition; MFI = Median Family Income; MD = Median; LH = Lower Hinge; UH = Upper Hinge

income (and less competitive) states and much tighter among the higher income (and highly competitive) states.

Examining Residuals

The difference between an observed value and a smoothed value is known as the *residual* value, the importance of which is shown by the following rearrangement of terms in the basic equation for the exploratory approach: rough = data - smooth. In other words, a set of residual values is the same as the rough, and because exploratory data analysis is an iterative process in which successive roughs are examined for evidence of additional smooth, the examination of residuals is a crucial part of the approach.

Fortunately, the techniques for examining residuals are no different from the ones used to examine the original data. The most basic technique is the *residual plot* in which the residual Y values are plotted on the verti-

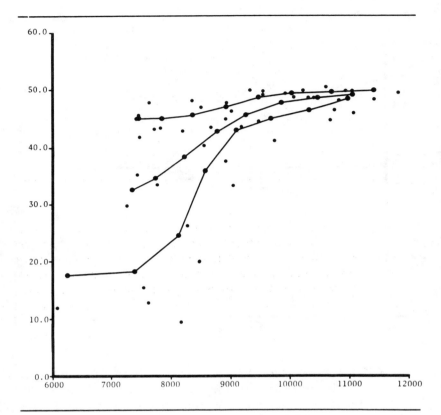

Figure 10

cal axis against the observed values along the horizontal (x) axis. To take the Democratic percentage of vote for President from 1896 to 1972 as an example, the residual values are determined by subtracting the smoothed values in the last column of Table 1 from the observed values in the second column. These values are then plotted against the same horizontal axis used in Figure 9, thus creating the residual plot shown in Figure 11.

A comparison of these two plots is instructive. Note first of all that observed values lying above the smooth in Figure 9 all have positive residual values, i.e., all lie above the dashed line in Figure 11. Note also that the farther above (or below) the smooth a value lies in Figure 9, the higher (or lower) its position in the residual plot in Figure 11. Thus, the second two Roosevelt victories, in 1940 and 1944, are considerably

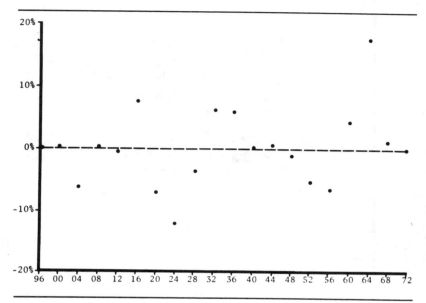

Figure 11

higher in the scatter plot than is Wilson's victory in 1916, but because they almost lie on the smooth, the Roosevelt percentages are located lower in the residual plot than is Wilson's percentage in 1916. In other words, Wilson's 49.24% was more unusual in the context of Presidential elections from 1896 through 1928 than were Roosevelt's 54.70% and 53.39% in 1940 and 1944. And notice also how Johnson's landslide in 1964 stands out in the residual plot. In comparison to the general decline in the fortunes of Democratic candidates for President since Roosevelt's 1936 landslide, Johnson's 61.05% of the total vote appears even more unusual than its position in the scatter plot indicates.

The residual plot for the Democratic vote for President displays the residuals from a data-generated smooth, but a plot of residual values from a straight line "first smooth" can also be instructive, particularly when the relationship is *non*linear. In fact, deviations from linearity are often more evident in the residual plot than in the original scatter plot because the residual values from a linear smooth contain everything in the original relationship *minus* whatever linearity exists in the relationship between the two observed variables.

This can be seen in Figure 12 which shows the residuals from a straight line fitted to the nonlinear relationship between median family

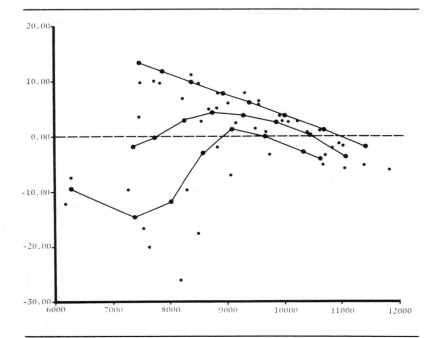

Figure 12

income and interparty competition shown in Figures 7 and 10. (Notice that because a residual plot is a type of scatter plot, median and hinge tracing can be done for residual plots as well as scatter plots of the observed variables.)

The primary reason for examining any residual plot is to see whether the rough is rough enough or whether it contains additional smooth, and this plot clearly shows additional smooth in the form of curvilinearity since the residual values start out negative, become positive in the middle range of X, and then become negative again in the upper range of X. In other words, a linear smooth has not removed all of the relationship between income and party competition in the United States, and this indicates the need to revise the initial model of the relationship, the initial smooth, and develop a nonlinear model which better fits the data, one which better describes the shape of the relationship and provides a better basis from which to measure the strength of the relationship.

The residual plot in Figure 12 also shows a second pattern in the residuals. The hinge traces show the spread of the residuals on Y decreasing with increases in the observed values on X, or what is known as *heteroscedasticity.* While the opposite, *homoscedasticity*, refers to a constant spread in the residuals throughout the range of X, heteroscedasticity refers to situations such as that in Figure 12, to a decreasing (or increasing) spread in the residual values associated with increasing values on X (see Lemieux, 1976).

In addition to examining the relationship between the residual values and the variable that forms the horizontal axis, it is often instructive to examine the *distribution* of the residuals. Ideally, the cases will tend to be concentrated along the smooth in the scatter plot, producing a concentration of residual values near the zero point in a stem-and-leaf, and there will be fewer and fewer cases as one moves away from the smooth, producing fairly symmetrical tails on each side of a single peak in the distribution. However, the stem-and-leaf display in Figure 13 shows a distinct right skew to the distribution and a disproportionate share of values in the +0 to +10 range, further evidence of the inappropriateness of a linear model of the relationship.

Understanding Relationships

Thus far a number of techniques have been presented which enable the data analyst to look at relationships between variables, but in order to understand relationships it is necessary not only to know how to look at relationships but also what to look for *in* the relationships. Although there are too many things to look for in relationships to be listed here in any exhaustive way, two things do stand out as important enough to warrant attention: (1) outliers and (2) nonlinearity (monotonic and nonmonotonic). Outliers and nonlinearity (of both types) are especially important because of their effect on the most common method of statistically summarizing relationships: least-squares linear regression. In each case, the use of least-squares linear regression, without visual examination of the relationship, not only can provide misleading summaries of one or more characteristics of the relationship but can also fail to reveal what may be the most important aspects of the relationship.

OUTLIERS

Relationships can have outliers just as distributions can, and just as outliers on a single variable are cases that are not part of the distribution of the other cases, so outliers in a relationship between variables

```
            +10 | 02368
             +5 | 01901988379
             +0 | 080062566869
             -0 | 45822259
             -5 | 393368
   FL,MS    -10 | 02
   LA,TX    -15 | 76
      SC    -20 | 1
      GA    -25 | 3
```

Figure 13

are cases that are not part of the relationship that exists among the other cases. An example of this is shown in Figures 8 and 14.

Outliers such as these are important because they can distort summaries of the relationship, as shown earlier in Figure 8, and this is particularly true when least-squares regression is used. Were one to rely on statistical summaries provided by least-squares regression, without visual examination of the relationship, one would conclude that only a weak negative relationship existed between the Democratic percentage of the vote by state in 1948 and 1952, as shown by the regression line R in Figures 8 and 14. In fact, however, a fairly strong *positive* relationship exists among 44 of the 48 states, as the same two figures show. Thus, the lack of resistance in the least-squares regression line leads to statistical summaries which are not only misleading but also fail to inform the data analyst about the most important characteristics of the relationship.

The easiest and most reasonable way to handle relationships such as these is to separate the outliers from the rest of the data. The outliers can then be analyzed separately and the remaining cases analyzed and summarized in terms of the shape, strength, and direction of the relationship that exists among them. This is an entirely reasonable way to proceed since the outliers are, by definition, not part of the same relationship as the other cases.

For example, a separate analysis of the four outliers in Figure 14 (Alabama, Mississippi, Louisiana, and South Carolina) shows the Republican candidate (Dewey) received 19.0%, 2.6%, 17.5%, and 3.8% of the vote in these states, while the Dixiecrat candidate (Thurmond) received 80.9%, 87.5%, 49.8%, and 72.0%. In other words, 1948 was a year in which a third-party candidate with a strong regional appeal took a substantial proportion of the vote away from the Democratic

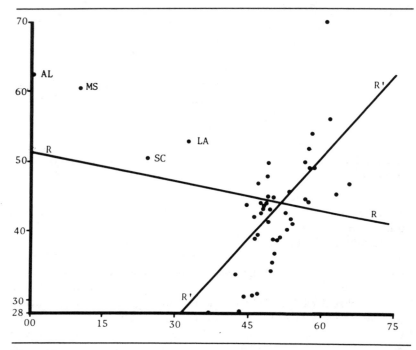

Figure 14

candidate in some of the Southern states, but without his appearance on the ballot in 1952, the Democratic candidate (Stevenson) was able to win a more normal percentage of the vote in these traditionally Democratic states.

The benefits in terms of the analysis of the other 44 states are shown in Figure 14; even the nonresistant least-squares regression line provides a workable summary when it is fitted to the remaining 44 states (R'). Not only does it fit the data better than the least-squares regression line for all 48 states (R) but also better than the highly resistant Tukey line for all of the cases (see line T in Figure 8). In short, setting aside the outliers for separate analysis has improved the analysis and understanding both of the outliers and of the remaining cases.

NONLINEAR MONOTONIC RELATIONSHIPS

Another important characteristic to look for in relationships is nonlinearity. First of all, some hypotheses, such as the Law of Diminishing

Returns, postulate a nonlinear relationship between variables, while other hypotheses, such as the relationship between income and inter-party competition, specify no particular shape for the relationship. In either case it is well worth a visual examination of the relationship to see whether, on the one hand, the nonlinear hypothesis is supported by the data or, on the other hand, there is an unexpected but nevertheless observable nonlinear relationship.

Second, least-squares linear regression *assumes* linear relationships between variables. This is not a hypothesis tested by linear regression, but an assumption on which it is based. It fits a straight line to the data no matter what the shape of the relationship and proceeds to summarize the relationship on that basis. Least-squares linear regression is a powerful statistical technique, but only if the relationship is, in fact, linear (and without outliers). If not, the statistical summaries it provides can be misleading and fail to convey information about the characteristic shape of the relationship.

Nonlinearity can take a wide variety of forms, but the distinction between monotonic and nonmonotonic relationships is most important. A monotonic relationship is one in which increases in X are associated either with increases in Y or with decreases in Y throughout the entire range of X. In other words, monotonic relationships do not double back on themselves. In contrast, nonmontonic relationships do double back on themselves, such as occurs whenever increases in X are associated with increases in Y up to some point, after which increases in X are associated with decreases in Y. Since all linear relationships are monotonic and all nonmonotonic relationships are nonlinear, three general classes of relationships exist: *linear, nonlinear monotonic,* and *nonmonotonic.* Nonlinear monotonic relationships differ from linear relationships in terms of the rate of increase or decrease. In linear relationships, the rate at which Y increases or decreases with increases in X remains the same throughout the entire range of X; hence, a straight-line relationship. In nonlinear but monotonic relationships, the rate at which Y increases or decreases along X changes. Increases in X may be associated with increases (or decreases) in Y at an increasing (or decreasing) rate, or even a combination of rates, but the direction of the relationship never changes. In contrast, nonmonotonic relationships are ones in which the direction itself changes.

An example of a nonlinear monotonic relationship is provided by the relationship between median family income and the Index of Inter-party Competition used in this section to demonstrate plots, traces, and residuals. As Figures 7, 10, and 12 all show, party competition increases with increases in median family income, but the increases occur at a decreasing rate. The slope of the median trace is steeper in the lower range of the income variable than it is in the upper range. What the plots seem to show is that party systems in the United States become more competitive as the level of income increases, but only up to a point. Because of the effective ceiling on the indices of inter-party competition imposed by the predominance of the two-party system, most states, even in the middle range of the income variable, have become competitive, and further increases in income then have only a marginal effect on the degree of party competition. In other words, the rate of increase decreases.

NONMONOTONIC RELATIONSHIPS

Relationships of this type are less common than monotonic ones, but they are not unknown. In fact, they sometimes appear in theoretical propositions. For example, Nagel hypothesizes that political discontent "will be lowest when important values are distributed most equally or most unequally; maximum discontent will ocuur at inter-mediate levels of inequality" (1974: 453). In other words, Nagel hypothesizes a change in the direction of the relationship; increases in equality will be associated will increases in political discontent up to a point, after which further increases in equality will be associated with *decreases* in discontent.

To test this hypothesis, Nagel used 1965 data for 26 South Vietnamese provinces (Russo, 1972). The horizontal axis in Figure 15 is 1.00 minus the Gini index of land tenure inequality, and the vertical axis is 1.00 minus an index of Saigon control in the provinces adjusted for several factors extraneous to the hypothesis. Thus, increases in the horizontal axis correspond to increases in equality, and increases in the vertical axis, to increases in political discontent.

As the scatter plot and median trace in Figure 15 show, the data support the nonmonotonic hypothesis. The relationship does, indeed, change direction; and political discontent is, in fact, lowest in those provinces with both the most and the least land tenure inequality. Thus, Nagel's research provides an example of both a nonmonotonic hypothesis and a nonmonotonic relationship in the data used to test the hypothesis.

For neither of these last two examples would linear regression be appropriate. Because the relationships are not linear, the numeric summary of the shape of the observed relationship (the linear regression equation) would be inaccurate, and because the shape of the relationship would not be modeled correctly, the correlation coefficient would

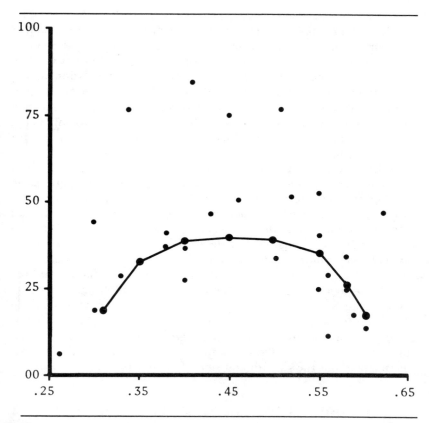

Figure 15

underestimate the strength of the relationship. Although the direction of the monotonic relationship would have been correctly summarized, the multiple directions of the nonmonotonic relationship would not have been. In short, linear regression cannot be used to numerically summarize observed relationships that are not linear.

SUMMARY

The techniques presented in this section for the analysis of relationships between variables differ from the more traditional techniques in two major ways: first, they are visual and, second, they are interactive. Because of the skepticism of numeric summaries of data, one of the principles which underlies the exploratory approach, relationships are examined by techniques which are less likely to mislead the data analyst, and because of the principle of openness, which also underlies the approach, exploratory data analysis emphasizes techniques which make it possible for the data analyst to discover the unexpected.

Statistical techniques such as least-squares linear regression are not rejected by the exploratory approach but, instead, they become part of a range of techniques, part of the "tool kit," if you will, of the data analyst. Statistical summaries may well be used, but only in conjunction with visual analysis and only when the summaries are appropriate for the data at hand.

From any perspective, the analysis of relationships is the process of dividing the data into the smooth and the rough, into patterns in relationships and deviations from the patterns; but from the exploratory perspective, this is an interactive process in which a first smooth is tried, the rough (i.e., the residuals) examined for evidence of smooth not included in the first pass at the data, the initial smooth revised to include any smooth discovered in the initial rough, the residuals from this new smooth examined for still more smooth, and so on until the rough is rough enough. In fact, the whole point of plotting, smoothing, and tracing is to enable the data analyst to develop an understanding of the empirical relationships by interacting with the data. Instead of simply feeding data into a computer and getting "answers" out at the end, the techniques presented in this section facilitate an interactive process of roughing out the smooth and smoothing out the rough.

4. LOOKING FOR STRUCTURE: REEXPRESSION

Introduction

Up to this point, skepticism about numeric summaries of variables and relationships between variables has been encouraged, as well as openness to the possibility that a variable may not have a normal distribution (symmetrical and single-peaked) and that it may not have a linear relationship to other variables. In fact, the previous two sections have been devoted to a series of techniques for visually representing data so they can be explored for various kinds of departures from normality and linearity. However, nothing has yet been said about what to do when such situations arise, and so this becomes the focus of the present section.

The key to handling problems created by nonnormality and nonlinearity lies in *reexpression*, a topic which we briefly discussed in the first section when we introduced the idea of using alternative scales in terms of log dollars. Reexpression is simply the use of a numeric scale of measurement other than the one on which a variable was originally recorded, and this is accomplished by transforming the observed data points by means of some arithmetic function.

Data are frequently collected by recording observations on an interval scale. That is, the unit of measurement is exactly the same size everywhere along the scale or, in other words, the intervals between logically adjacent points are equidistant, as in the case of measuring the pitch of sound in terms of cycles per second.

The use of interval scales implies that equal intervals have significance but, in fact, this is not always the case. In the example of sound, the interval between 110 cycles per second (cps) and 220 cycles per second is the same distance as that between 440 and 550 cps; after all, is not an interval of 110 cps always 110 cps? Not necessarily. In fact, the musical scale postulates that the interval between 110 and 220 cps has exactly the same significance as the interval between 440 and 880 cps. Even though the latter is four times the former, each interval is one octave, as shown in Figure 16. In fact, a piano keyboard is a logarithmic reexpression of the physical scale of cycles per second on which the pitch of sound is measured.

The important point is not the concept of an octave, but that of reexpression; and what this particular reexpression does is to alter the distance between the points along the scale while at the same time maintaining the sequence, or order, of the points. In transforming cycles per second into notes on a keyboard, distances are shrunk at the upper end of the physical scale relative to those at the lower end by means of the $\log_2$ function. The same distance of 110 cps represents a smaller and smaller distance the higher one goes on the keyboard, or in other words, larger and larger differences in cycles per second are necessary in order to achieve the same octave difference on the musical scale. Notice, however, that the order of the "data" is preserved: 440 cps is a higher pitched note than 220 cps, and 220 cps is a higher pitched note than 110 cps.

It may now be clear why reexpression is an important way to handle nonnormal distributions. Consider, for example, the distribution of the Index of Interparty Competition depicted in the section on single-variable distributions (Figure 4) and compare the box-and-whisker there with the one shown in Figure 17. The cases at the lower end of the distribution of the original indices are too far apart relative to those at the upper end, but by decreasing the distances at the lower end of the distribution (or increasing those at the upper end), the trans-

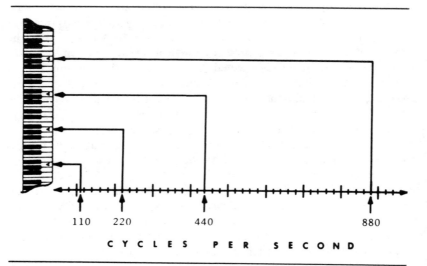

110   220   440   880

C Y C L E S   P E R   S E C O N D

Figure 16

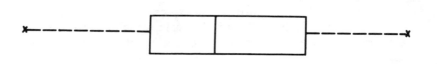

Figure 17

formation Wright (1975) developed symmetrizes the skewed distribution characteristic of the original Index of Interparty Competition.

What is not so clear is that reexpression can also linearize scatter plots. Indeed, it might be thought that nonnormality and nonlinearity are independent of each other and that a transformation responding to the nonnormality of a variable would have nothing to do with non-linear relationships, or that, in fact, it might make relationships with other variables even more nonlinear. However, *nonnormality and non-linearity often go hand in hand* and, because of this, *reexpression is a useful response to both problems.*

To understand why, it is necessary first to make a distinction between linear and nonlinear transformations. Adding, subtracting, multiplying, and dividing a variable by a constant, or any combination of these operations, will not only preserve the order of the data points but also the relative distances between them, and because of this the shape of the distribution will not be affected. Moreover, a plot of the new values against the original ones will be a straight line; hence the term *linear transformation*. In contrast, transforming a variable by logs, roots, powers, and exponentials will change relative distances between data points, thereby producing distributions with different shapes, and, because of this, nonlinear scatter plots are produced when the transformed data points are plotted against the original ones. Hence the term *nonlinear transformations*.

In these terms, the linear regression equation produces a set of predicted ($\hat{Y}$) values that is a linear transformation of the observed X values since the equation $\hat{Y} = a + bX$ simply multiplies X by one constant and adds another. Therefore, the shape of the distribution of the $\hat{Y}$ values will either be the same as that of the X values or, if the relationship is negative, the shape of one will be the mirror image of the other. Thus, for the relationship between X and Y to be linear, they must have similar (or mirror image) distributions.

Conversely, if the shape of the distribution of Y differs substantially from that of X, the relationship cannot be linear since no transformation, including the linear regression equation, could map the distribution of X into the distribution of Y; the only kind of transformation which could is a *non*linear transformation. In other words, the relationship between X and Y must be nonlinear, for given two dissimilar distributions, such as a symmetrical and a skewed distribution, it is impossible to draw a scatter plot which is both linear and satisfies the constraints imposed by the two distributions. This is not to say that the relationships between variables with similar distributions must, of necessity, be linear, but only that distributions with dissimilar distributions *cannot* be linear.

The relationship between median family income and the Index of Interparty Competition can be used to demonstrate these points. The median family income values have a symmetrical distribution; the Index of Interparty Competition has an asymmetrical, left-skewed distribution; and as would be predicted, the relationship between them is nonlinear, as shown in Figures 7, 10, and 12. However, by using Wright's symmetrizing reexpression of the Index of Interparty Competition, the distributions of the two variables in the relationship become similar and, as shown in Figure 18, the relationship becomes linear. The cases clustered at the top of the original scatter plot are spread out vis-a-vis those at the bottom, and this has the effect of moving the main cluster of cases in the middle range of the income variable downward, thereby straightening the relationship.

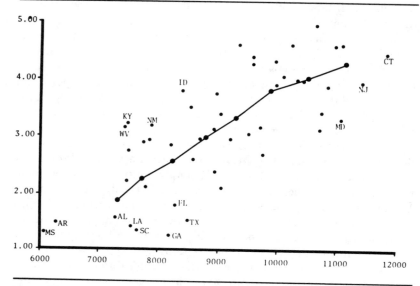

Figure 18

Thus, reexpressing the Index of Interparty Competition has not only removed skewness from the distribution but it has also led to a linear relationship between the symmetrically distributed median family income values and the reexpressed Index of Interparty Competition.

Not all instances of nonlinearity are so tractable, primarily because similarity in distributions does not insure linearity in the relationship between variables. However, reexpression remains the cornerstone of the exploratory approach to data analysis because it is an important response to both nonnormality in distributions and nonlinearity in relationships. In fact, reexpression often responds to both conditions simultaneously, as it did in the example of median family income and interparty competition.

This linkage between the shape of distributions and the shape of relationships offers the basis for a systematic approach to modeling nonlinear relationships. As a matter of procedure, *the data analyst should begin by symmetrizing the distributions of variables* and then use the *symmetrized* variables in further analysis. The reasons for this are twofold. First, if all variables have symmetrical, single-peaked distributions, then nonlinearity caused by distributions with divergent shapes will be eliminated. This will not eliminate all cases of nonlinearity, but the most common forms can be handled in this way, and any remaining nonlinearity can be more easily modeled once the variables have been symmetrized.

Second, symmetry is a desirable property in itself. First of all, the details of distributions and of relationships are easier to see when the data are not concentrated in one area. In a stem-and-leaf or box-and-whisker, a disproportionate clustering of cases in one range makes it difficult to determine the important properties of the distribution of the bulk of the cases, as in Figure 5, and a disproportionate clustering of cases in one segment of a scatter plot makes it difficult to see the relationship that is characteristic of most of the cases, as in Figure 8.

Second, even resistant summaries of the location and spread of distribtions can be misleading when the distributions are not symmetrical, as shown by the untransformed Index of Interparty Competition in section 2, and since numeric summaries of the strength of relationships are based on measures of location and spread, they, too, can be misleading when the variables are not symmetrical.

Third, as we have already shown, estimates of location and spread are highly dependent upon the shape of the distribution; and, in particular, the mean-variance combination often used to estimate the parameters of location and spread behaves quite poorly when asymmetrical distributions are involved. Only for symmetrical distributions with moderate tails do the alternative estimators of the location and spread of a distribution converge, while for more asymmetrical and long-tailed distributions, the values obtained for various estimators vary considerably. In addition, there is something bizarre in describing the location of a distribution at a point larger than all but a few data points (as in the case of the mean within a right-skewed distribution) or the spread as so large that over 90% of the data points are included (as in the case of the variance in the asymmetrical case). Especially when comparing results of alternative fits to some relationship, which is normally done by an explained variance criterion, the estimates of location and spread should be reasonable.

Thus, symmetrizing distributions of variables by means of reexpression prior to the analysis of relationships between variables not only contributes to the analysis of nonlinear relationships but also provides a solid basis for measures of explained variance and statistical significance. Although the relationship between two variables with right-skewed distributions (for example) may be linear, reexpressing both variables in terms of a symmetrizing transformation will not alter the linear relationship, and it will provide a more solid basis for any regression analysis techniques that may be used to summarize the relationship.

Choosing Reexpressions

Not every mathematical function is equally useful as a reexpression in exploratory data analysis. Other things being equal, simple transformations are preferable to more complex ones. However, the simplicity of a function is not determined by the number of arithmetic operations, but by the effect of the operations on the original values.

Three characteristics of a set of values can be identified: the numerical values themselves, the relative distances between them, and the rank order of the values. The more of these characteristics that are affected by reexpression, the more complex is the function which generates the reexpression. (It should be noted that simply reversing the sequence of values does not change the order. The order of the values is not scrambled but preserved; it is just reversed.)

In terms of this typology, linear functions are the most simple since they only affect the numerical values. For example, a set of values can be reexpressed in terms of standard deviations from the mean, i.e., "standardized," by subtracting the mean from each value and dividing by the standard deviation. Unless the mean of the original values is zero and the standard deviation is one, the reexpressed variable will have different numerical values. However, the relative distances between the cases will have been preserved, as well as their rank order.

In contrast, squaring a set of positive numbers will not only assign different numerical values but it will also change the relative distances between them. The distance between cases at the high end of the distribution will have been increased relative to the distance between cases at the low end. However, the cases will still have the same rank order. The higher a case ranked on the original scale, the higher it will rank on the new scale.

The most complex functions affect all three characteristics of a set of values. Squaring a variable which includes both positive and negative numbers will not only affect the numerical values themselves and the relative distances between them, but since both X and $-X$ will become X^2, the ordering of the cases will be affected as well. Squaring the values -4, 2, and 3 changes the order; the lowest value (-4) becomes the highest (16), while the middle value (2) becomes the lowest (4) and the highest (3) becomes the middle value (9).

Two major distinctions between arithmetic functions are indicated by these three types of changes: that between linear and nonlinear functions and that between monotonic and nonmonotonic functions. A monotonic function is one that does not change the order of cases, while a nonmonotonic function does, and within the category of monotonic functions, linear ones do not alter the relative distances between cases, while nonlinear ones do. Thus, since all linear functions are monotonic and all nonmonotonic functions are nonlinear, three categories arise. They are, in order of complexity: *linear, nonlinear monotonic*, and *nonmontonic*.

The interrelationship between the reexpression of variables and the development of alternative models of an observed relationship between variables should now be obvious. If the relationship is linear, then it can be modeled by a linear reexpression of X, and this is precisely what linear regression does. If the observed relationship is nonlinear but monotonic, it can be modeled by a nonlinear monotonic reexpression of X, or of Y, or perhaps both. In other words, nonlinear monotonic relationships can be modeled by reexpressions which simply adjust relative distances between values on either or both variables. Nonmonotonic relationships, however, require reexpressions which change the order of the data points in order to model changes in the direction of the relationship. In short, they require nonmonotonic functions.

NONLINEAR MONOTONIC FUNCTIONS

Within the class of nonlinear monotonic functions there are two major types: *concave* and *convex*. Concave functions receive their name because they face downward and are concave (like a lens) toward the larger values, as shown in Figure 19. What is interesting about these functions is what they do to distances at various ranges. Note that the horizontal distance between points a and b on the original scale is equal to that between c and d, but after the concave transformation is applied, a′ and b′ on the vertical axis are clearly farther apart than c′ and d′. Consider, then, what happens when data are bunched up on the left side of a distribution with some outliers on the right. A concave transfromation spreads out these lower (left-hand) values relative to the outliers on the right or, in other words, a concave transformation "pulls in" the outliers on the right. This effect is shown in the box-plots in Figure 19.

Convex functions are the opposite of concave functions. They face the opposite direction, as the name suggests, and they have the opposite property with respect to distances in various ranges. Distances in the upper range of the original scale are magnified, while those in the lower range are reduced. Thus, convex functions are useful when the data points are bunched on the right side of a distribution since they will spread these out while "pulling in" data points on the left. The shape

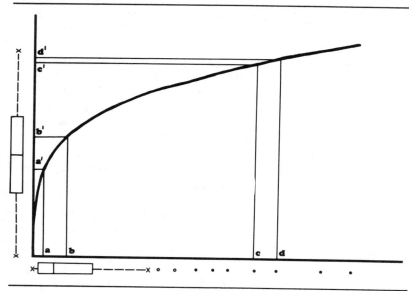

Figure 19

of convex functions and their impact on left-skewed distributions is shown in Figure 20.

The two most useful concave functions are natural logarithms and the family of roots (square roots, cube roots, quadratic roots, and so on), while the most useful convex functions are exponentials and powers.

It is important to note that the impact of concave and convex functions varies along the curve formed by the function. For example, the effect of power functions on the shape of a distribution increases with the magnitude of the numbers involved. Therefore, it is sometimes necessary to adjust the original values beforehand by means of a linear transformation in order to use just the right portion of the curve, "right" in the sense of having neither too much nor too little effect on the shape of the distribution. Thus, it may be necessary to increase or decrease the magnitude of the values by adding or subtracting a constant or to expand or contract the range by rescaling the values. Moreover, it may be necessary to eliminate negative numbers by adding a constant in order to make use of a nonlinear function at all, as in the case of logarithms, or to avoid nonmonotonic transformations, as in the case of powers.

Rescaling is a linear reexpression which involves setting the smallest observed value equal to the minimum value of the new scale, the largest

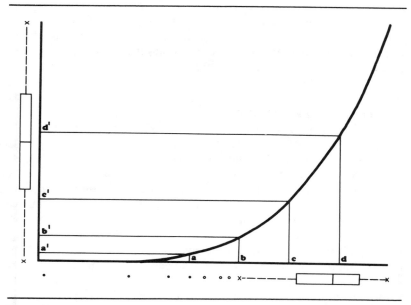

Figure 20

observed value equal to the maximum value in the new scale, and fitting all other values in between while maintaining the relative distances between them. For example, by subtracting the lowest value from each of the observed values and dividing the remainders by the range of the observed values, a variable can be easily rescaled so it ranges between zero and one. For many purposes, however, zero and one have undesirable properties, particularly when logs and roots are to be used. For example, the log of zero is undefined, and any root of 1.00 is still 1.00. For this reason, the rescaled values may be multiplied by a constant slightly less than 1.00, such as .990, with a value equal to one-half of 1.00 minus the constant then added, such as .005. The result is a linear reexpression of the original variable into a range less then 1.00, from .005 to .995 in this example and, by doing this, the peculiarities of zero and one can be avoided.

Thus, linear functions may be combined with nonlinear montonic functions in order to symmetrize the distribution of a variable, but any complexity is more apparent than real. The important part of the function is the nonlinear part; the linear portion is a convenient means of exploiting the useful range of the nonlinear function.

The value of concave and convex functions lies in their ability to reexpress a skewed variable in terms of a scale along which the variable is symmetrically distributed. However, even symmetrical distributions do not necessarily approximate the shape of a normal distribution. They may have too many cases concentrated in the middle of the distribution, resulting in "stretched" tails, or they may lack tails altogether, or even have a concentration of cases in the tails themselves, resulting in a U-shaped distribution.

Suppose a distribution has outliers on both sides, in other words, stretched tails. In this case, ordinary concave and convex functions are only half right; they fix one side of the distribution but only make the other side worse. What is needed is a transformation that is convex to the left and concave to the right, one that has the effect of *icing the tails*, in the vernacular of exploratory data analysis. There are several transfromations which are convex on the left and concave on the right, the most important of which are the sine function and the odd-numbered roots. To use any of these functions, it is necessary first to set the median of the original data equal to zero since this is the point at which these kinds of functions change from convex to concave. This is done by subtracting the median from each of the data points. In the case of the sine function, it is also necessary to rescale the data so that they lie within the monotonic range of the function. This is done by multiplying the observed values by a constant that guarantees that neither the largest nor the smallest value extends beyond $\pm\pi/2$. Application of the sine function to these rescaled values then brings in the outliers on both sides of the distribution. The shape of this function and its effects are shown in Figure 21.

Suppose a distribution has the opposite of stretched tails, that it has fat tails with too many values located at the extremes. In this case, a function is needed which has the opposite effect from icing the tails, something which spreads out the values concentrated in the tails, in other words, pulls values in toward the middle of the distribution. What is needed is a transformation that is concave on the left and convex on the right.

As in the case of icing the tails, there are several transformations which have the desired properties: odd-numbered powers, folded logs (*flogs*), and folded roots (*froots*). For odd-numbered powers, the data must be rescaled so that the median equals zero for the same reason that this must be done when icing the tails. However, a more complicated rescaling must be done before a froot or a flog is used.

To obtain either folded logs or folded roots, it is necessary first to rescale the original values from a point just above zero to a point just below 1.00, e.g., from .005 to .995. Folded logs are then obtained by applying the following equation to these rescaled values: $1/2 \log_e$

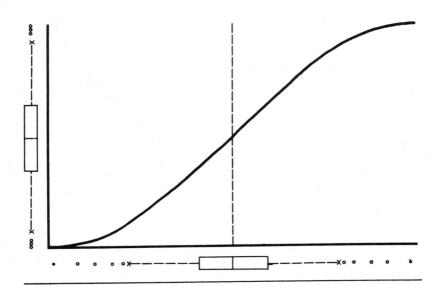

Figure 21

$X - 1/2 \log_e (1 - X)$, where X is the rescaled value for each case, and folded roots are obtained by applying the following equation to the rescaled values; $\sqrt{2X} - \sqrt{2(1 - X)}$. The "log" and "root" portions of the terms are obvious. The "folding" occurs as a result of subtracting the log (or root) of $1 - X$ from the log (or root) of X. The shape of this type of function and its effects are shown in Figure 22.

The preceding discussion has described one method for modeling a nonlinear monotonic relationship, namely, reexpressing one or both of the variables in terms of a scale of measurement on which it has a symmetrical, single-peaked distribution. An alternative method is to look at the shape of the relationship (e.g., the median trace) and choose a function that has the same shape as the relationship. The range of functions given in the preceding discussion is a basic set, to which may be added such functions as $1/X$ and the logit: $X/1 - X$ where X is a frequency.

Since inferential regression statistics are based on a normal distribution of the dependent (Y) variable, every effort should be made to symmetrize the dependent variable. In particular, if it is skewed, it should be symmetrized, and if it is already symmetrical, then the independent (X) variable alone should be reexpressed. If the latter is desired, one can select the function directly from the picture. For example, a scatter plot

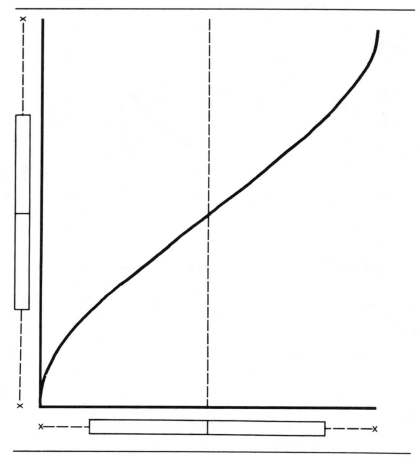

Figure 22

with a median trace that looks like Figure 19 would dictate a log or root transformation on the independent variable since log and root functions have concave shapes. On the other hand, if it is the dependent (Y) variable that is to be transformed, the inverse of the function that is pictured should be used, i.e., the function which would *de*transform the one that is pictured. For example, one would apply an exponential or power transformation to the dependent variable in order to model a relationship that has a median trace like Figure 19.

These two approaches to modeling nonlinear monotonic relationships do, however, tend to converge. If one of the variables has a distribution which approximates the shape of a normal distribution, the same type of function that will normalize the nonnormally distributed variable will also have the same shape as the relationship between the two variables. This can be shown by the example of median family income and interparty competition, even though it would initially seem to contradict the convergence of the two approaches. The median trace of the relationship has the same concave shape as the log and root functions, but a log transformation of the Index of Interparty Competition was used even though, according to the guidelines just stated, the *inverse* of the log function should have been used since it was the dependent variable that was reexpressed. However, Wright used the log function *prior* to reflecting the Index of Interparty Competition. Thus, before reflection, the shape of the relationship was that shown by the median trace in Figure 9, but upside down, i.e., sloping downward and to the right at a decreasing rate. To model a relationship of this shape, one might use a negative exponential, the inverse of which is a negative log. Thus, the log transformation Wright used prior to reflection is also the inverse of the shape of the relationship between the two variables prior to the reflection of the Index of Interparty Competition. All that reflection of the index does is remove the negative sign in the relationship, thus showing a positive relationship between median family income and the degree of party competition.

NONMONOTONIC FUNCTIONS

The convergence of normalizing distributions and modeling the shape of nonlinear monotonic relationships does not, unfortunately, apply in the case of nonmonotonic relationships. In fact, nonmonotonic functions should never be used to normalize distributions since nonmonotonic functions preserve none of the characteristics of the original variable: not the observed values, the relative distances, or even the order of the cases. About all one is left with is the name of the original variable. Nonetheless, nonmonotonic functions are sometimes necessary in order to model, and to describe, those relationships which change direction, such as the one shown in Figure 14.

The question, then, is how best to model such relationships, and there are basically two techniques for doing this. The first is to look at the median trace of the relationship, or even the pairs of smoothed median values used to generate the median trace, and then try to figure out a mathematical function that will describe the relationship. For example, were the smoothed medians on X equal to 0, 25, 60, 60, 130, and 140 and the smoothed medians on Y equal to 5625, 2500, 225, 225, 3025, and 4225, the follwoing function would describe the relationship between the two sets of values: $Y = (X - 75)^2$. Having described the median trace, this function would also describe the relationship between X and Y, but even this relatively simple example serves to demonstrate the difficulty of determining what function would describe the relationship between the two variables.

The alternative is to use polynomial regression. The general equation for polynomial regression is $\hat{Y} = a + b_1 X + b_2 X^2 + b_3 X^3 + \ldots + b_k X^k$. The advantage of polynomial regression is its ability to put nonmonotonic bends in a regression line, i.e., generate a regression line that doubles back on itself. Moreover, the polynomial regression equation can be treated incrementally. Notice that the "first degree" polynomial regression equation, the one with only the $b_1 X$ term in it, is also the linear regression equation and, of course, it generates no bends in the regression line. The "second degree" polynomial regression equation ($\hat{Y} = a + b_1 X + b_2 X^2$) will generate one bend; the "third degree" polynomial regression equation will generate two bends, and so on.

As a general rule, one should use the polynomial regression equation one degree higher than the number of changes in direction (number of bends) in the relationship. Applying this to the example of equality and political discontent in the 26 South Vietnamese provinces means the use of the second degree polynomial equation, i.e., the regression of the index of political discontent on the reflected Gini index of land tenure inequality (1.00 − Gini index) and the square of the reflected Gini index. If polynomial regression has modeled the relationship, then the residual plot should not contain the upside down U shape that characterized the scatter plot in Figure 14 and, as shown by Figure 23, this is, in fact, the case. The median trace of the plot is not completely flat, but it is about as flat as one can expect with only 26 data points and, in any case, the nonmonotonic relationship between equality and political discontent has been removed, in other words, modeled by the polynomial regression equation.

Summary

The major point of this section has been the efficacy of reexpressing variables in order to symmetrize distributions of individual variables and to model relationships between variables that are not linear. Unfortunately, it is not possible to state precise rules by which to choose reexpressions, but it is possible to provide some useful guidelines.

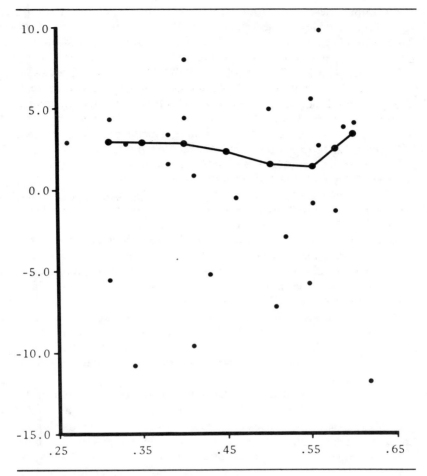

Figure 23

First, nonnormally distributed variables and nonlinear monotonic relationships (ones in which the rate but not the direction of relationship changes) can be handled by reexpressions which adjust relative
distances between values while preserving their rank order. Nonmonotonic relationships (ones in which both the rate *and* the direction
change) require either nonmonotonic reexpression or polynomial
regression.

Second, among the nonlinear monotonic reexpressions there are
three main types: concave, convex, and such hybrids as the sine function, **odd-numbered** roots and powers, and folded roots and logs. The

choice among these types should depend upon the shape of the distributions of the variables. To be specific, the function or functions which are chosen should symmetrize any asymmetrical distributions. By doing so, most nonlinear monotonic relationships will be modeled, and the symmetrical, single-peaked distributions of the variables will provide a better basis on which to compute such regression statistics as the percent of explained variance. In some cases, particularly those involving several changes in the rate at which increases (or decreases) in Y are associated with increases (or decreases) in X, normalizing functions may not remove all of the structure in the relationship. In these cases, X should be further reexpressed with a function that has the same shape as the median trace of the residual plot.

Choosing particular functions within each type, say a log function versus a quadratic root, can be a matter of theoretical choice, trial and error, or both. Certainly substantive considerations should be used when they apply (log dollars make more sense than quadratic root dollars), but when no substantive considerations apply or the function chosen on a substantive basis does not work, it frequently requires more than one interaction with the data before a function is found which removes the structure in the relationship.

Finally, models of relationships developed by this approach sometimes *appear* to defy substantive interpretation. For example, what theory could possible explain a relationship in which $\hat{Y}_i = a + b \log [.990$ $((X_i - \min)/(\max - \min)) + .005]$ where min is the lowest value and max is the largest value on X?

The interpretation of such models requires that they be broken into their components. One is the "data manipulation" component. In the example above, the subtraction of the minimum value, the division by the range, the multiplication by .990, and the addition of .005 are simply data manipulations, just as the subtraction of the mean and division by the standard deviation to create "standardized" variables are data manipulations. The second component is the nonlinear function(s), the log term in the example above, or the sine function in icing the tails; and the third component, the linear regression component, consists of the regression coefficient and the constant term.

The linear regression component often has substantive importance, but it is not the part of the model that causes difficulty in theoretical interpretation.

The data manipulation component often appears to be complex, but it is not normally important in any substantive sense, nor is it necessary to explain it in theoretical terms. One would not expect any theory to explain why one subtracted the means from a set of X and Y values and then divided by the standard deviations whenever one used standardized variables in linear regression. Data manipulation only makes it possible to exploit that portion of the nonlinear function which is most useful in modeling the particular observed relationship. In fact, were data manipulation all there were to the model, the relationship would simply be linear.

This leaves the nonlinear component, which involves two considerations: the specific function and the type of function. In some cases the specific function may be substantively important, whether it is a log function or a root function, but in most cases what is important is the *type* of function, whether it is concave, convex, or what. In these terms, what the example used above is saying is that the relationship between X and Y is concave, that increases in X are associated with increases in Y at a decreasing rate. Thus, by analyzing apparently complex models in terms of their components, it becomes possible to develop substantive interpretations of the models.

5. MULTIVARIATE ANALYSIS: PUTTING IT ALL TOGETHER

In a typical empirical research project, one defines the subject to be studied, collects appropriate data, analyzes the data, and comes to some substantive conclusions as a result of the analysis. In arguing for a data-centered approach based on openness to alternative models and skepticism about numerical summaries, the previous three sections have presented both univariate and bivariate techniques to aid the researcher in understanding the nature of the variables being used and the relationships between the variables. Typically, however, the researcher seeks to understand not just relationships between two variables, but relationships among sets of variables, in other words, *multivariate* relationships.

In a real sense, univariate techniques are a prelude to bivariate techniques, and these, in turn, lay the groundwork for multivariate analysis, for developing a multivariate model of the data. The question, then, is how one approaches this sort of modeling within the exploratory perspective.

The answer does not lie in such techniques as factor analysis or stepwise regression or, for that matter, any approach which is not interactive and which places too much reliance on nonresistant numeric summaries of the data. Instead, the exploratory approach emphasizes a step-by-step visual approach to understanding the structure of each variable, then each pair of variables, and finally, groups of variables. In other words, the approach is incremental because each step in the analysis is based upon the understandings developed from the previous step. This is obviously a more time-consuming approach to multivariate analysis, but it is also more instructive, both because the researcher has had to *interact* with the data and because later decisions are less likely to be based on false assumptions.

This is not to say that exploratory analysis does not make use of any multivariate numeric summaries. In fact, it does, including multiple linear regression (see Blalock, 1972; Hayes, 1973; or Kmenta, 1971). This form of refression analysis is like simple (bivariate) linear regression in most respects, but the multiple linear regression equation makes the predicted $\hat{Y}$ values a function of more than one variable: $\hat{Y} = a + b_1X_1 + b_2X_2 + \ldots + b_kX_k$. Instead of forming a straight line through two dimensional space, the $\hat{Y}$ values form a straight line through n-dimensional space where there are as many dimensions as there are variables in the model. Residual values (the rough) are still computed in the same way $(Y_i - \hat{Y}_i)$; the line is still located so as to minimize the sum of the squared residual values (least squares); and the coefficient of (multiple) determination is still determined the same way as it is in simple linear regression. Thus, multiple linear regression is a natural multivariate extension of bivariate linear regression.

Though multivariate statistical techniques are used in exploratory data analysis, they are not used at the beginning of the data analysis process or are multivariate modeling decisions allowed to be made on the basis of linear assumptions and numeric summaries of the data. Rather, the exploratory approach to multivariate analysis involves the following steps:

(1) Each variable should be thoroughly understood and symmetrized.
(2) Relationships between all pairs of variables should be thoroughly understood and linearized.
(3) Multivariate relationships should be built from bivariate relationships by adding additional explanatory variables which smooth successive roughs.
(4) Causal implications should be drawn from the relationships between pairs of roughs.

Step 1: Univariate Analysis

The researcher should begin the data analysis by visually and numerically inspecting the distribution and noting the shape of each variable. When necessary, variables should be reexpressed so as to symmetrize their distributions. It should be determined what monotonic transformation is required to make the shape of the distribution of the bulk of the cases "bell-shaped," while any outliers which are not part of the overall shape of the distribution should be identified by case name and either left in the data set and carefully watched in further analysis or set aside for separate analysis. In no case should the distribution of the rest of the cases be distorted in behalf of the outliers. In short, using the techniques presented in section 2, the researcher should develop an understanding of the structure of each variable and, if necessary, reexpress variables in preparation for bivariate analysis.

Step 2: Bivariate Analysis

The next step is to examine the relationships between pairs of variables, thus beginning to understand the network of relationships which characterize the data set. Since asymmetrical distributions and nonlinear relationships often go hand in hand, the bivariate relationships may already be linear in terms of the reexpressed variables. However, if any nonlinearity is apparent in scatter plots using the reexpressed variables, the horizontal variable should be appropriately transformed.

Step 3: Multivariate Analysis

To develop multivariate relationships, the researcher starts with a relationship from step 2 and obtains the residuals. These residuals are then plotted against variables which are expected to explain some of the remaining structure. In other words, a multivariate model is constructed by successively extracting structure from the residuals with new variables, and when additional smooth cannot be extracted from the final rough, the multivariate model is completed, at least as far as possible with the existing data set.

An example of this is provided by Nagel's analysis of political discontent in the South Vietnamese provinces. The "adjusted index" of political discontent referred to in earlier discussions of this example is actually 1.00 minus the set of residual values from a multiple linear regression of the percentage of hamlets under Saigon control in each of the provinces on five other variables. These residuals are, thus, the rough that remains after the first five variables have accounted for as much structure as possible. In an effort to extract further smooth from this rough, the residuals were plotted against a sixth variable, the measure of land tenure equality (1.00 minus the Gini index of *in*equality).

This produced the scatter plot shown in Figure 14, and as the example went on to show in section 3, the smooth in the relationship was modeled by the use of polynomial regression.

After building a multivariate model by this incremental method, the final check is to examine a plot of the residual values from the model against the values predicted by the multiple linear regression equation. The reason for this is that the residuals cannot be plotted against X, as in simple linear regression, because there is more than one X variable. However, the predicted values are a linear reexpression of the X variables combined by weighting them according to the regression coefficients, the $b_i X_i$ values, and therefore any structure that remains in this residual plot indicates structure remaining in the multivariate relationship between Y and one or more of the X variables.

Step 4: Causal Analysis

In addition to multivariate relationships, one may also be interested in partial relationships, i.e., relationships between two variables while controlling, or holding constant, one or more of the other variables. Relationships of this type have particular importance whenever one is trying to make inferences about the causal relationships between variables, in other words, causal modeling (Asher, 1976; Blalock, 1961; Duncan, 1975; Heise, 1975).

For example, one might theorize that social welfare expenditures are not only higher in states that have more competitive party systems but also that the greater degree of party competitiveness is one of the *causes* of the higher level of welfare expenditures (see, for example, Dawson and Robinson, 1963; and Cnudde and McCrone, 1969). However, it is also true that wealthier, more economically developed states have highly competitive party systems *and* that they have high levels of welfare expenditure. Therefore, the fact that welfare expenditure levels are high in states with competitive parties is not sufficient reason to infer that party competition causes high levels of welfare expenditure. It is entirely possible that the relationship is not a causal one, but that it is spurious, i.e., that the relationship between high levels of party competition and high levels of welfare expenditure may be the result of both variables having a common source in high levels of wealth. They may only be related because the wealthier, more economically developed states have both highly competitive parties and high welfare expenditures. This spurious model is shown in diagram form in Figure 24.

If the results of the bivariate analyses in the second step show that measures of all three factors are interrelated—in other words, that

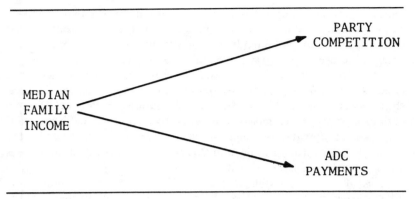

Figure 24

median family income, the Index of Interparty Competition, and welfare expenditures, measured by the average monthly Aid to Dependent Children, ADC, payments per recipient family (U.S. Bureau of the Census, 1971), are each related to the other two variables—and this is actually the case, then the problem is to sort out the partial relationships and to see whether party competition might be causally related to ADC payments when the effect of differences in income levels is removed.

In order to do this, the relationships between income and party competition and between income and ADC payments must first be correctly modeled. The failure to model any nonlinear relationships at this stage can be particularly damaging to causal inferences at later stages because the full effect of the control variable, income in this example, will not have been removed. If, for example, the relationship between income and party competition is not linear but concave, as it is in this example, sole reliance on a linear model of the relationship will not remove all of the structure in the relationship and, as a result, not all of the effect of differences in income levels on differences in levels of party competition will have been removed. The control variable will not have been completely controlled; there will continue to be a relationship between the two variables, albeit not a linear one. Thus, the analysis of partial relationships is highly dependent upon a careful analysis and correct modeling of bivariate relationships in order to remove fully the effects of the control variable.

Once relationships between the control variables and the variables whose causal relationship is being examined have been correctly modeled, the next step is to obtain the residuals for the two variables. These constitute the rough, the variation in the two variables that remains, that is unexplained by or not attributable to the control variable. Therefore, if the two sets of residual values are related, then the two variables for which they are the residuals must be related even when the effects of the control variable are removed. In other words, the relationship between the residuals is the partial relationship between the two variables when the effects of the control variable are held constant. Thus, any relationship between the residuals cannot be attributed to the effect of the control variable, and this is what makes causal inferences about such relationships possible.

It is, of course, possible to attribute the partial relationship to the effect of one or more variables which have not been controlled, but the key assumption behind all causal modeling is that all relevant variables have been included in the model. If this is not the case, then no causal inferences can be drawn. However, should additional variables be brought forth as potentially accounting for the partial relationship, they can be included in a somewhat more complex model and the partial relationships reexamined.

For example, one might argue that party competition and ADC payments are also affected by the degree of urbanization and the degree of industrialization. To take both of these into account along with median family income, the partial relationship between party competition and ADC payments would need to be examined while controlling for the effects of all three variables.

This requires going back to the first step and examining the distribution of the two additional variables, and also going back to the second step and examining the relationships between the additional variables and each of the original three variables. What this shows in this example is that the percentage of the population living in urban areas (the measure of urbanization) and the percentage of employed persons not engaged in farming, fishing, or forestry (the measure of industrialization) are both left-skewed and that exponential reexpression of both variables symmetrizes their distribution after a linear transformation of the former by dividing by 100.0 and a linear transformation of the latter by dividing by 5.0. These reexpressions also have the effect of creating linear relationships between each of the additional variables and the original three variables.

The next step is to regress both party competition and ADC payments on the three control variables and examine the scatter plot created by the two sets of residuals, in other words, the partial relationship between party competition and ADC payments shown in Figure 25.

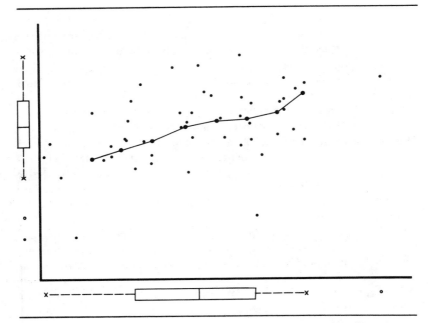

Figure 25

What this scatter plot shows is a relationship between the two sets of residuals that is basically linear, i.e., a linear partial relationship and, because of this, the two numerical summaries used in causal analysis are appropriate: the partial correlation coefficient and the standardized regression coefficient, or path coefficient. The former is simply the correlation coefficient expressing the strength of the relationship between the two sets of residuals, .197 in this example, and the latter is the regression coefficient for the same relationship multiplied by the standard deviation of the independent variable (the reexpressed Index of Party Competition) divided by the standard deviation of the dependent variable (the ADC payments), or .413 in this example. On the basis of these two coefficients, as well as the relationship shown in the scatter plot, there appears to be a causal relationship between party competition and ADC payments in the United States, or at least the relationship between them cannot be explained in terms of differences in the level of economic development, and that is all one can expect from causal modeling.

The exploratory approach to multivariate analysis is no different from the exploratory approach to univariate and bivariate analysis. The underlying point in all three is to "get to know your data."

Data analysis should be a confrontation between theory and data, but for this to be effective, the researcher needs to be as familiar with the data as with the theory. Unfortunately, much data analysis in the social sciences relies so heavily on numerical summaries of the data that these summaries intervene *between* the researcher and the data, often shielding the researcher *from* the data.

The exploratory approach is basically a way of thoroughly examining the data by *looking* at the data, and often looking at *all* of the data, e.g., the stem-and-leaf and the scatter plot, and by doing this, the researcher is able to develop a better understanding of the data. This can have two consequences, corresponding to the basic equation in the exploratory approach: data = smooth + rough. First, one can develop a better understanding of the smooth in the data that, for example, the percentages of national populations that are literate tend toward the extreme values of 0% and 100% and slope toward the middle forming a U-shaped distribution, or that the relationship between median family income levels in the United States and the level of party competition has a nonlinear, concave shape. Second, one can develop an understanding of the rough in the data that, for example, 4 states do not fit the same pattern as the other 44 states in the relationship between the vote for Truman in 1948 and the vote for Stevenson in 1952, and that the specific states are Alabama, Mississippi, South Carolina, and Louisiana. Numerical summaries often rely on assumptions about the data, such as normality in distributions or linearity in relationships. However, by exploring the data, one does not have to make simplifying and sometimes erroneous assumptions and, of course, numerical summaries cannot provide a description of that which is not summarized, namely the rough. Yet both the smooth and the rough can be instructive in testing and developing empirical theories about the social world.

6. THE EXPLORATORY PERSPECTIVE REVISITED

The preceding sections have concentrated on techniques which facilitate the exploration of data but, as set forth at the onset, the use of these techniques does not by itself make one an exploratory data analyst. In particular, the reader is cautioned against applying exploratory techniques with the same rigidity of thought that characterizes much traditional data analysis. Exploratory data analysis is interactive and iterative. There is no invariant procedure by which the exploratory data analyst takes a data set and automatically generates *the* smooth and *the* rough. Indeed, different exploratory data analysts may legitimately employ different techniques and even find different structures in the same set of data.

The principles of openness and skepticism permeate the exploratory data analyst's methodology. He or she is skeptical even of resistant statistics and visual summaries, as in the case of median and box-and-whisker for U-shaped distributions such as national literacy rates, and he or she questions the very accuracy of the raw data, as in the case of railroad mileage per square mile of land in Cuba. The exploratory data analyst is also open to potentially revealing alternative displays, summaries, and reexpressions of the data. In short, the exploratory analyst develops a smooth from the data by examining successive roughs with an open mind and a variety of visual and numerical techniques.

This is not to say the exploratory data analyst is adrift without a compass in a sea of data. Just as explorers both of earth and space have a guiding rubric, so does the exploratory data analyst. The great explorers of man's physical surroundings struck a delicate balance between following a charted course and remaining open to the unexpected, and so it is with the exploratory data analyst.

The course followed by an exploratory data analyst, while open to modification en route, can be outlined as follows:

(1) Understand each variable as a separate entity.
(2) Understand pairs of variables as relationships.
(3) Understand groups of variables as models.

The first step in understanding one's data is to understand the structure of each variable. Using such techniques as the resistant number summary, stem-and-leaf display, and box-and-whisker plot, one should understand where the distribution is located, how spread out it is, and what its shape looks like. Any outliers or gaps in the distribution should be noted, as well as multiple peaks and skewness.

If the shape of the distribution can be adequately symmetrized by some nonlinear monotonic transformation, the variable should be reexpressed, but when reexpressing at this early stage, it is important neither to disort the basic shape of the distribution to accommodate a few highly deviant cases nor to alter the order of the data by nonmonotonic transformations. Care must be taken to insure that reexpression does not mislead the analyst later in the analysis.

Once individual variables have been carefully examined, scatter plots, traces, and/or smoothers such as the Tukey line or the 53R'H should be used to examine pairs of variables for nonlinearity not already removed by reexpression motivated by the univariate analysis. If the shape of the smooth in a relationship between variables is not linear, but can be summarized by reexpression(s) of the independent and/or dependent variable by some linearizing transformation, the variable(s) should be reexpressed, but as in the case of univariate analysis, reexpression should not distort the smooth to accommodate a few deviant cases.

The examination of relationships between pairs of variables should not be limited to an examination of the smooth, but the rough as well by taking deviations from the smooth, i.e., the residuals, and subjecting them to the same careful examination given to the observed (or reexpressed observed) values. Then, the rough can be examined for evidence of additional smooth. In this way, the data analyst can be sure he or she is aware of and understands all of the important structure in the relationship.

Once the smooth (perhaps expressed by some linearizing reexpression) and the rough (perhaps including outliers) have been examined for pairs of variables, multivariate modeling can be undertaken. Multivariate models are built iteratively from the examinations of successive roughs, and causal inferences are drawn from relationships between pairs of roughs.

In the final analysis, the data analyst seeks to understand the network of relationships in the data, but rather than attack the problem all at once, the analyst breaks it down into manageable pieces: first understanding each variable, then each important bivariate relationship, then finally the network of multivariate relationships in the data. This is not a rigid course of action leading to some inexorable conclusion, but a plan of attack to be custom-fitted to the data at hand. Nonetheless, at each step visual summaries and displays, resistant numeric summaries, and reexpression are the tools with which the data analyst develops a coherent picture of the data at hand.

It should also be emphasized that exploratory data analysis tends to suggest rather than confirm hypotheses, and it can even be argued that the exploratory data analyst forfeits the right to test the statistical significance of any models that are generated since they are not *a priori* hypotheses in the statistical sense. However, the exploratory state of mind and the exploratory techniques need not be limited to situations in which the researcher is theoretically adrift. Many times research begins with only partial theories, i.e., theories which do not specify all *three* characteristics of relationships, and in such situations, an exploratory approach to the analysis of data can fill in such gaps in the theory as the shape of relationships. But even when the researcher is engaged in full-scale theory testing, or the replication of previous work, an openness to alternatives, a healthy skepticism, and a tool box of useful reexpressions, displays, and summaries can be beneficial. Indeed, expecting the unexpected is the hallmark of a good data analyst.

Finally, this monograph does not describe the gamut of exploratory techniques. There are, for example, methods for analyzing contingency tables and categorical data that employ the same principles expounded here, as well as additional techniques for exploring the kinds of data used in the preceding sections. For a discussion of additional techniques, the reader should consult Tukey (1977), Mosteller and Tukey (1977), and McNeil (1977).

REFERENCES

ANDREWS, D. F. et al. (1972) Robust Estimates of Location: Survey and Advances. Princeton: Princeton Univ. Press.

ANSCOMBE, F. J. (1973) "Graphs in statistical analysis." Amer. Stat. 27 (February): 17-21.

ASHER, H. B. (1976) Causal Modeling. Beverly Hills: Sage.

BANKS, A. S. (1971) Cross-Polity Time Series Data. Cambridge: MIT Press.

BLALOCK, H. M., Jr. (1972) Social Statistics. New York: McGraw-Hill.

——— (1961) Causal Inferences in Nonexperimental Research. Chapel Hill: Univ. of North Carolina Press.

BOX, J.E.P. and B. R. COX (1964) "An analysis of transformations." J. of the Royal Stat. Soc. (Series B) 27: 211-243.

CNUDDE, C. F. and D. M. McCRONE (1969) "Party competition and welfare policies in the American states." Amer. Pol. Sci. Rev. 63: 858-866.

Congressional Quarterly (1975) Presidential Elections since 1789. Washington, DC: Author.

DAWSON, R. E. and J. A. ROBINSON (1963) "Inter-party competition, economic variables, and welfare policies in the American states." J. of Politics 25: 265-289.

DUNCAN, O. D. (1975) Introduction to Structural Equation Models. New York: Academic Press.

GROSS, A. M. (1976) "Confidence interval robustness with long-tailed symmetrical distributions." J. of Amer. Stat Assn. 71: 409-416.

HAMPEL, F. R. (1978) "Contributions to the theory of robust estimation." Ph.D. dissertation, Univ. of California at Berkeley.

HARTER, L. H. (1969) Order Statistics and Their Use in Testing and Estimation (Vol. 2). Washington, DC: U.S. Government Printing Office.

HAYES, W. L. (1973) Statistics for the Social Sciences. New York: Holt, Rinehart & Winston.

HEISE, D. R. (1975) Causal Analysis. New York: John Wiley.

HUBER, D. R. (1975) "Robust statistics: a review." Annals of Math. Stat. 43: 1041-1067.

KMENTA, J. (1971) Elements of Econometrics. New York: Macmillan.

KRUSKAL, J. B. (1968) "Transformations of data." International Encyclopedia of the Social Sciences (Vol. 15): 182-193.

LAX, D. A. (1975) "An interim report of a Monte Carlo study of robust estimators of width." Technical Report No. 93 (Series 2). Dept. Statistics, Princeton Univ.

LEINHARDT, S. and S. S. WASSERMAN (1979) "Exploratory data analysis: an introduction to selected methods." Soc. Meth.: 311-365.

LEMIEUX, P. H. (1976) "Heteroscedasticity and causal inference in political research." Pol. Methodology 3: 287-316.

McGILL, R., J. W. TUKEY, and W. A. LARSEN (1978) "Variations of box plots." Am. Stat. 32 (February): 12-16.

McNEIL, D. R. (1977) Interactive Data Analysis: A Practical Primer. New York: John Wiley.

MOSTELLER, F. and J. W. TUKEY (1977) Data Analysis and Regression: A Second Course in Statistics. Reading, MA: Addison-Wesley.

NAGEL, J. H. (1974) "Inequality and discontent: a nonlinear hypothesis." World Politics 26: 453-472.

PFEIFFER, D. G. (1967) "The measurement of inter-party competition and systematic stability." Amer. Pol. Sci. Rev. 61: 457-467.

RUDDLE, K. and M. HAMOUR (1973) Statistical Abstract of Latin America, 1972. Los Angeles: Univ. of California.

RUSSO, A. J., Jr. (1972) "Economic and social correlates of government control in South Vietnam," in I. K. Feierabend et al. (eds.) Anger, Violence, and Politics. Englewood Cliffs, NJ: Prentice-Hall.

STALLINGS, B. (1972) Economic Dependency in Africa and Latin America. Beverly Hills: Sage.

TAYLOR, C. L. and M. C. HUDSON (1972) World Handbook of Political and Social Indicators. New Haven: Yale Univ. Press.

TUFTE, E. R. (1974) Data Analysis for Politics and Policy. Englewood Cliffs, NJ: Prentice-Hall.

——— (1969) "Improving data analysis in political science." World Politics 21: 641-654.

TUKEY, J. W. (1977) Exploratory Data Analysis. Reading, MA: Addison-Wesley.

——— and M. B. WILK (1970) "Data analysis and statistics: techniques and approaches," in E. R. Tufte (ed.) The Quantitative Analysis of Social Problems. Reading, MA: Addison-Wesley.

U.S. Bureau of the Census (1973) Census of Population 1970 (Vol. 1). Characteristics of the Population Part 1, United States Summary—Section 1. Washington, DC: U.S. Government Printing Office.

——— (1971) Statistical Abstract of the United States: 1971. Washington, DC: U.S. Government Printing Office.

——— (1954) Statistical Abstract of the United States: 1954. Washington, DC: U.S. Government Printing Office.

VELLEMAN, P. F. (1976) "Robust non-linear data smoothers: definitions and recommendations." Economic and Social Statistics Technical Report 776-001. Dept of Economic and Social Statistics, New York State School of Industrial and Labor Relations, Cornell Univ.

WRIGHT, G. C., Jr. (1975) "Interparty competition and state social welfare policy: when a difference makes a difference." J. of Politics 37: 796-803.

GLOSSARY

BOX-AND-WHISKER: A visual summary of the distribution of a single variable which provides detail whenever one or both of the tails of a distribution contain unusually large or small values. See Figures 4, 5, and 16.

CONCAVE FUNCTIONS: Nonlinear monotonic reexpressions which pull in outliers on the high end of a distribution and spread out values on the low end. Used to symmetrize right-skewed distributions. See Figure 18.

CONFIRMATORY MODE: A mode of analysis in which numeric summaries generated by imposing an a priori model on the data are used either to confirm or disconfirm a hypothesis.

CONVEX FUNCTIONS· Nonlinear monotonic reexpressions which pull in outliers on the low end of a distribution and spread out values on the high end. Used to symmetrize left-skewed distributions. See Figure 19.

EXPLORATORY MODE: An interactive and iterative mode of analysis in which both numeric and visual summaries and displays are used to explore data for unanticipated patterns. Characterized by openness and skepticism.

53R′H: A smoothing technique using running medians of group five, repeated running medians of group three, copied end values, and hanning. Particularly useful for time-series data. See Table 1 and Figure 8.

FLOG (FOLDED LOG): A reexpression which spreads out values concentrated in the tails of a distribution. Used when the tails of a distribution are abnormally short.

FROOT (FOLDED ROOT): Also a reexpression which spreads out values concentrated in the tails of a distribution. See Figure 21.

HANNING: A smoothing technique in which the average of every pair of adjacent numbers in a sequence is computed, followed by the average of every adjacent pair of averages just computed, with end values copied from the original sequence. Frequently used as the final smooth after repeated running medians. See Tables 1 and 2.

HIGHSPREAD: The numeric distance between the median and the highest value in a distribution. The range of the upper half of the data.

HINGE (LOWER): The point above which three-fourths and below which one-fourth of the values lie in a distribution.

HINGE (UPPER): The point above which one-fourth and below which three-fourths of the values lie in a distribution.

ICING THE TAILS: Pulling in both tails of a distribution which has extreme values on both ends. Includes the use of either the sine function or odd-numbered roots after setting the median of the distribution equal to zero and rescaling the original values so none exceeds $\pm\pi/2$. See Figure 20.

LOCATION: The point at which a distribution is anchored; the point around which the values are distributed. Often measured by the mean, median, or mode, though the median is usually preferred in exploratory analysis because of its resistance.

LOWSPREAD: The numeric distance between the median and lowest value in a distribution. The range of the lower half of the data.

MIDSPREAD: The numeric distance between the lower hinge and the upper hinge in a distribution. The range of the middle half of the data. Also equal to the width of the box in a box-and-whisker plot.

NONMONOTONIC (FUNCTION): Any arithmetic function which reexpresses a variable in such a way that it changes not only the original values and the relative distances between them but also the order of the original values. Includes, for example, squaring a set of values with both positive and negative numbers.

NONMONOTONIC (RELATIONSHIP): Any relationship between variables that changes direction, that doubles back on itself, at least once. See Figure 9 and 15.

NONLINEAR MONOTONIC (FUNCTION): Any arithmetic function which reexpresses a variable in such a way that it changes the original values and the relative distances between them, but does not change the order of the original values. Includes concave and convex functions, as well as those which spread out or pull in extreme values in both tails of a distribution.

NONLINEAR MONOTONIC (RELATIONSHIP): Any relationship between variables in which the rate of increase or decrease changes at least once, but not the direction of the relationship. See Figure 10.

OPENNESS: One of the two major principles underlying the exploratory approach to data analysis. A willingness to explore data for unanticipated patterns by reexpressing variables and developing a smooth from the data themselves.

OUTLIER: In a distribution, any case which lies outside the normal range of the data, i.e., lies well above or well below most, or even all, of the other cases. See Figure 5. In a relationship, any case which is not part of the relationship that exists among the bulk of the cases, i.e., lies well above or well below a resistant smooth of the relationship. See Figure 8.

REEXPRESSION: The use of numeric scale of measurement other than the one on which the variable was originally recorded. Accomplished by transforming the observed data points by means of some arithmetic function. Used to reduce the problems of nonnormality and nonlinearity.

RESCALING: Any linear reexpression which sets the smallest observed value equal to the minimum value of the new scale, the largest observed value equal to the maximum value, and all other observed values in between while maintaining the relative distances between them. Usually precedes nonlinear monotonic or nonmonotonic reexpression in order to make the later reexpression effective.

RESIDUAL PLOT: A visual display of the rough in which each case is represented by a dot directly above its observed value on the horizontal axis and directly opposite its residual value on the vertical axis. Useful for examining the relationship between the independent variable and the rough on the dependent variable. See Figures 11, 12, and 24.

RESIDUALS: The differences between the observed values and the smoothed values; the rough.

RESISTANCE: That property of some smoothing techniques (e.g., the Tukey line) and some measures of location and spread (e.g., the median and midspread) which makes them relatively impervious to the effects of outliers.

ROUGH: Deviations from the smooth, from patterns in the data. Whatever is left behind when the smooth is removed from the data; the residuals, for example.

RUNNING MEDIANS: A smoothing technique in which medians are determined for a series of overlapping groups of a constant but odd-numbered size. For groups of three, the median of the first three values in a sequence is determined, the next value in the sequence is included, the first one excluded, and the median of the new but overlapping group determined, and so on through the last three values. See Tables 1 and 2.

SCATTER PLOT: A visual display of the relationship between variables in which each case is represented by a dot directly above its value on the horizontal axis and directly opposite its value on the vertical axis. Useful for examining the direction, strength, and especially shape of relationships. See Figure 7.

SKEPTICISM: One of the two major principles underlying the exploratory approach to data analysis. The unwillingness to accept without question summaries of the major characteristics of distributions and relationships, particularly numeric summaries.

SLICING: The division of the data points in a relationship into a series of nonoverlapping groups (slices) along the horizontal axis. The first step in median and hinge tracing.

SMOOTH: The underlying, simplified structure in a set of observations; the pattern(s) in the data. For example, a line passing through the data points in a relationship and conforming to the general shape and direction of the relationship. See Figures 9, 10, 15, and 20.

SMOOTHING: Any process by which the smooth is identified in the data. For example, the 53R'H procedure by which trends are identified in time-series data.

SPREAD: The variablity of a set of values; the width of a variable; how spread out the cases are. Often measured by the standard deviation, though the midspread is usually preferred in exploratory analysis because of its resistance.

STATISTICS: Numeric summaries of the characteristics of either distributions or relationships, such as means, medians, standard deviations, midspreads, regression coefficients, correlation coefficients, and so on.

STEM-AND-LEAF: A visual display of the distribution of a variable. Resembles a histogram. Each case is represented by one or more digits to the right of a vertical line and in the row corresponding to the first digit(s) of the observed value. See Figures 2, 3, and 15.

TRACES (MEDIAN AND HINGE): Lines connecting the smoothed cross-medians and cross-hinges from a sliced relationship. A smoothing technique used to summarize the shape of the smooth and the rough in a relationship. See Figures 10, 12, 15, 19, 25, and 27.

TUKEY LINE: A resistant linear smoother. A straight line fitted to a relationship by finding the cross-medians of the first one-third and last one-third of the cases along the horizontal axis and moving the line connecting the cross-medians parallel to itself until one-half of the cases lie above and one-half below the line can also be located arithmetically. Useful as a first smooth to remove linearity from a relationship so the residuals from the line can be examined for evidence of nonlinearity.

FREDERICK HARTWIG, Associate Professor of political science at Union College, Schenectady, New York, received his B.A. degree in government from Lawrence College and his M.A. and Ph.D. degrees in political science from Northwestern University. He has written articles appearing in Political Methodology *and* Behavioral Science.

BRIAN E. DEARING, Advanced Programmer at the Telecommunications and Information Processing Operations of the General Electric Company, graduated from Union College as valedictorian with a major in political science.

G-3190

Name _____

Address _____

City _____ State _____ Zip _____

☐ I want to take advantage of your **Prepaid Special Offer.**
☐ Please send me all 93 papers at the **prepaid** price of **$665.88**
☐ Please send me the 10 papers checked below at the special **prepaid** price of **$71.60**
My check or money order is enclosed.

This Special Offer is available in the U.S. and Canada only.
Special Offers Expire August 31, 1993.
☐ Please send me the Sage Papers checked below at the regular price of $8.95 each.

$8.95 each

Quantitative Applications in the Social Sciences

A SAGE UNIVERSITY PAPERS SERIES

SPECIAL OFFERS
(for **prepaid** orders only)

Order all 93 for $665.88 and save over $165.00

or

Order any 10 papers for $71.60 and save over $17.00

Orders under $30 must be prepaid. California residents add 7.25% sales tax. All prices subject to change without notice.

On prepaid orders, please add $2.00 handling charge.

SAGE PUBLICATIONS

☐ 1 Analysis of Variance, 2nd Ed. *Iversen / Norpoth*
☐ 2 Operations Research Methods *Nagel / Neef*
☐ 3 Causal Modeling, 2nd Ed. *Asher*
☐ 4 Tests of Significance *Henkel*
☐ 5 Cohort Analysis *Glenn*
☐ 6 Canonical Analysis and Factor Comparison *Levine*
☐ 7 Analysis of Nominal Data, 2nd Ed. *Reynolds*
☐ 8 Analysis of Ordinal Data *Hildebrand / Laing / Rosenthal*
☐ 9 Time Series Analysis, 2nd Ed. *Ostrom*
☐ 10 Ecological Inference *Langbein / Lichtman*
☐ 11 Multidimensional Scaling *Kruskal / Wish*
☐ 12 Analysis of Covariance *Wildt / Ahtola*
☐ 13 Introduction to Factor Analysis *Kim / Mueller*
☐ 14 Factor Analysis *Kim / Mueller*
☐ 15 Multiple Indicators *Sullivan / Feldman*
☐ 16 Exploratory Data Analysis *Hartwig / Dearing*
☐ 17 Reliability and Validity Assessment *Carmines / Zeller*
☐ 18 Analyzing Panel Data *Markus*
☐ 19 Discriminant Analysis *Klecka*
☐ 20 Log-Linear Models *Knoke / Burke*
☐ 21 Interrupted Time Series Analysis *McDowall / McCleary / Meidinger / Hay*
☐ 22 Applied Regression *Lewis-Beck*
☐ 23 Research Designs *Spector*
☐ 24 Unidimensional Scaling *McIver / Carmines*
☐ 25 Magnitude Scaling *Lodge*
☐ 26 Multiattribute Evaluation *Edwards / Newman*
☐ 27 Dynamic Modeling *Huckfeldt / Kohfeld / Likens*
☐ 28 Network Analysis *Knoke / Kuklinski*
☐ 29 Interpreting and Using Regression *Achen*
☐ 30 Test Item Bias *Osterlind*
☐ 31 Mobility Tables *Hout*
☐ 32 Measures of Association *Liebetrau*
☐ 33 Confirmatory Factor Analysis *Long*
☐ 34 Covariance Structure Models *Long*
☐ 35 Introduction to Survey Sampling *Kalton*
☐ 36 Achievement Testing *Bejar*
☐ 37 Nonrecursive Causal Models *Berry*
☐ 38 Matrix Algebra *Namboodiri*
☐ 39 Introduction to Applied Demography *Rives / Serow*
☐ 40 Microcomputer Methods for Social Scientists, 2nd Ed. *Schrodt*
☐ 41 Game Theory *Zagare*
☐ 42 Using Published Data *Jacob*
☐ 43 Bayesian Statistical Inference *Iversen*
☐ 44 Cluster Analysis *Aldenderfer / Blashfield*
☐ 45 Linear Probability, Logit, Probit Models *Aldrich / Nelson*
☐ 46 Event History Analysis *Allison*
☐ 47 Canonical Correlation Analysis *Thompson*
☐ 48 Models for Innovation Diffusion *Mahajan / Peterson*
☐ 49 Basic Content Analysis, 2nd Ed. *Weber*

☐ 50 Multiple Regression in Practice *Berry / Feldman*
☐ 51 Stochastic Parameter Regression Models *Newbold / Bos*
☐ 52 Using Microcomputers in Research *Madron / Tate / Brookshire*
☐ 53 Secondary Analysis of Survey Data *Kiecolt / Nathan*
☐ 54 Multivariate Analysis of Variance *Bray / Maxwell*
☐ 55 The Logic of Causal Order *Davis*
☐ 56 Introduction to Linear Goal Programming *Ignizio*
☐ 57 Understanding Regression Analysis *Schroeder / Sjoquist / Stephan*
☐ 58 Randomized Response *Fox / Tracy*
☐ 59 Meta-Analysis *Wolf*
☐ 60 Linear Programming *Feiring*
☐ 61 Multiple Comparisons *Klockars / Sax*
☐ 62 Information Theory *Krippendorff*
☐ 63 Survey Questions *Converse / Presser*
☐ 64 Latent Class Analysis *McCutcheon*
☐ 65 Three-Way Scaling and Clustering *Arabie / Carroll / DeSarbo*
☐ 66 Q-Methodology *McKeown / Thomas*
☐ 67 Analyzing Decision Making *Louviere*
☐ 68 Rasch Models for Measurement *Andrich*
☐ 69 Principal Components Analysis *Dunteman*
☐ 70 Pooled Time Series Analysis *Sayrs*
☐ 71 Analyzing Complex Survey Data *Lee / Fortholer / Lorimor*
☐ 72 Interaction Effects in Multiple Regression *Jaccard / Turrisi / Wan*
☐ 73 Understanding Significance Testing *Mohr*
☐ 74 Experimental Design and Analysis *Brown / Melamed*
☐ 75 Metric Scaling *Weller / Romney*
☐ 76 Longitudinal Research *Menard*
☐ 77 Expert Systems *Benfer / Brent / Furbee*
☐ 78 Data Theory and Dimensional Analysis *Jacoby*
☐ 79 Regression Diagnostics *Fox*
☐ 80 Computer-Assisted Interviewing *Saris*
☐ 81 Contextual Analysis *Iversen*
☐ 82 Summated Rating Scale Construction *Spector*
☐ 83 Central Tendency and Variability *Weisberg*
☐ 84 ANOVA: Repeated Measures *Girden*
☐ 85 Processing Data *Bourque / Clark*
☐ 86 Logit Modeling *DeMaris*
☐ 87 Analytic Mapping and Geographic Databases *Garson / Biggs*
☐ 88 Working with Archival Data *Elder / Pavalko / Clipp*
☐ 89 Multiple Comparison Procedures *Toothaker*
☐ 90 Nonparametric Statistics *Gibbons*
☐ 91 Nonparametric Measures of Association *Gibbons*
☐ 92 Understanding Regression Assumptions *Berry*
☐ 93 Regression with Dummy Variables *Hardy*

1/93

Sage Publications, Inc.
P.O. Box 5084, Newbury Park, California 91359
PHONE: (805) 499-0721 / FAX: (805) 499-0871

Quantitative Applications in the Social Sciences

(a Sage University Papers Series)

$8.95 each

SAGE PUBLICATIONS, INC.

P.O. BOX 5084

NEWBURY PARK, CALIFORNIA 91359—9924

Place
Stamp
here